The 40-Day Human Detox

The 40-Day Human Detox

A Path to Healing, Inner Peace, and Self-Discovery

Dr. Theresa Pepcee' Edwards

Printed in the United States of America

Paperback ISBN: 979-8-9917761-6-5

Cover art by Janika.

Publishing Services:
Tucker Publishing House, LLC
11000 W. McNichols Rd.
Suite 323
Detroit, MI 48221
www.tuckerpublishinghouse.com

TABLE OF CONTENTS

DEDICATION

This book is dedicated to my beloved children, Shontenique, Jamyrin, and Mariah, and my precious grandchildren, Emir, Erik, and Erron. You are the reason I continue to fight, grow, and persevere. Thank you for giving my life purpose and meaning.

ACKNOWLEDGEMENTS

I am deeply grateful to my family and friends for their unwavering belief in me. A heartfelt "thank you" to my sisters, Sachi Lewis and Charnice Alexander, my best friends, Dawn Johnson, Antionette Ousley, and Kendra Washington.

Special appreciation to my cousin, Britney Austin-Ingram, for always pushing me forward.

I sincerely thank Prinder Mitchell for inviting me to share my story and my best friend, Patrick Garth, for continually encouraging me to do so.

I want to give a special acknowledgment to Coach Tara of Tucker Publishing House. Your visionary leadership, professionalism, and dedication transformed my dream into reality and exceeded all my expectations.

FOREWORD

It is a privilege to write this foreword for Dr. Theresa Pepcee' Edwards and her remarkable book, The 40-Day Human Detox: A Path to Healing, Inner Peace, and Self-Discovery. In a time when words are plentiful but meaning often seems lacking, Dr. Edwards has created a timely and timeless book—a testament to her keen insights and unwavering passion.

When I first encountered Dr. Edwards and her work, I was struck by her unique ability to weave profound insights into her human life experience and how it shaped her through an authentic and profoundly engaging voice. This book reflects her dedication to helping others heal and the footprint their new growth will bring.

The 40-Day Human Detox: A Path to Healing, Inner Peace, and Self-Discovery is more than a collection of ideas or stories; it invites us to think differently, feel deeply, and engage more meaningfully with ourselves and the world. Dr. Edwards's approaches are a testament to the power of human resilience, shared knowledge, and inspiration, reminding us that we are all part of a more extraordinary tapestry in which every thread has its purpose.

It has been an honor to witness the evolution of this work—through personal conversations, shared experiences, or simply as an admirer of her growth and resilience. I can confidently say that what lies within these pages is a gift to everyone who opens it. Whether new to Dr. Edwards's work or a long-time follower, this book will resonate with you, provoke thought, and leave an impression.

As you embark on your journey through The 40-day Human Detox: A Path to Healing, Inner Peace, and Self-Discovery, I encourage you to take your time. Allow the words to resonate with you and carry their lessons as you progress. Within these pages lies the potential to inspire and transform you, leaving a lasting impact long after you finish reading.

Thank you, Dr. Edwards, for sharing this work. Thank you, dear reader, for opening your heart and mind to it.

Warm regards,
Dr. Kenneth Coleman

Scan the QR Code for an Audio Introduction

INTRODUCTION

"I must find a way to fight for
my life and seek a way to change."

Wounds have a way of taking you to dark places within your thoughts, mind, and soul. You feel smothered, drowning in an unexplainable space, fighting for the strength to be better. With each heartbeat, you close your eyes to try and make sense of where your mind is taking you. You pause, and you begin to say positive things to yourself; you pray, you exercise because this has worked in the past. But yet, here you are again, feeling overtaken by insurmountable pain from a wound that you thought healed.

Recurring pain can alter how you think, feel, view, and approach life. Your decision-making becomes challenging, and you question your self-worth and, in some instances, your reason for existence. At times you may feel stuck and unable to move forward. Let go of the past, forgive, and give yourself another chance.

At one point in my life, I became accustomed to pain; this was my normal life. I began to believe that I was supposed to be unhappy due to all of the trauma I experienced by the age of 9. I would say to myself, "Why did God let *me* be born?" Through my teenage years, things became worse. I was homeless at 14 years old. I would think, "How is this possible?" Then, in my early 20s I was shot in the leg with a 9mm. I was convinced my life was meant to be horrible.

Every year was not bad. I have accomplished great things in my life. However, the pain that showed up unannounced always made me feel like I was sinking. It felt as if I was standing in a dark hole deep below the ground. I would look up and see a small speck, and that was the sky. I would imagine pulling myself up the sides of the walls. If I could just get to the top, I could breathe and see that things would change.

Over the years, I learned how to face my hurt and forgive. I would embrace life, be thankful, and do things that made me happy. But, that was not enough. I still had moments of feeling emotionally overwhelmed for no particular reason. Just a throbbing pain in my heart, a soreness that I could not massage or treat.

This was my experience of how pain, wounds, and scars were in my life.

Some things never heal.
Some pain never leaves.
Some thoughts never erase.
Some emotions never subside.
…despite it all…
I have a purpose and a reason to exist.

Why did I write this book?

The unexpected hurt. The unexplainable pain. The constant throb. It appears without cause, without reason, without a trigger. Each time, I clench my chest, my eyes water, my breathing is calculated, my mind is racing, and I am in despair because I do not understand the "Why." *Why* does this continue to happen? *Why* do I have this knot of pain that shows up whenever it wants to?

A stabbing, radiating pain from broken relationships, failures, loneliness, and physical, sexual, and verbal abuse causes a large, uncomfortable cramp in my chest. It would hurt to breathe. I said to myself, "This is the last time that I will feel this pain." I needed to find a different approach than before; I wanted a new way because everything I tried only worked temporarily.

I decided to go on a 40-day human detox. A journey of exploration of self. To travel through my life and experiences so that I could authentically understand who I had become. I promised myself that I would be honest and dedicated to doing the work.

At the end of my 40-day human detox, I learned that I needed emotional support to feel important and relevant in my relationships. I discovered that this craving came from my childhood and life experiences. As a result, I am now able to comfortably express this to anyone in my life. More importantly, I no longer experience that excruciating pain.

I wrote this book because I want you to find peace and healing from your pain. Nothing's for certain, and there are certainly no guarantees, but if there is an opportunity to help someone, I have to share. I started my 40-day human detox without knowing the end result. I am glad I took that leap of faith because I am worth the change and so are you!

This book is for those seeking answers to their pain. Those who want to try a new approach to gain a different perspective about themselves and how to address their needs. God gave me this quote… "I have to know the definition of myself before I can define myself to others." Part of knowing myself is knowing my pain, of being vulnerable and courageous enough to share my needs with others.

In the pages of this book, you will find affirmations, words of wisdom, and learn how journaling helps you process and self-reflect. This is a deep dive into the parts that are hidden from the world—the parts you keep hidden from yourself. It is important to know your triggers so when they arise, or when you are presented with a situation that makes you want to fight, flight, or be a fawn, you address it in that moment. You will gain an immeasurable understanding of yourself, thus impacting your life and the lives of those around you. To assist with gaining a deeper understanding, I also have a companion journal. You can get a copy here: **www.40dayhumandetox.com.**

Honesty matters. You cannot lie to yourself. You have done that enough. I am open and transparent to show you that it is okay. Your deliverance is important to achieving a greater level of self-awareness. Healing past the camouflage and the mask to get there will not be easy. No worries, because I am going on this journey with you.

How to use this book:

I have set it up so that you can use it on your own or join me, and we can journey together. Each detox begins with an audio intro-duction, which you can hear by scanning the QR code.

Each day is a detox. It is important to affirm yourself; therefore, each detox will begin with an affirmation, a theme, and an inspirational quote. There will be a daily reflection, and a personal transparent story, followed by reflection prompts. You cannot end without taking action, so I have action steps for you. This combined recipe is the 40-day human detox. You may choose to use the book over 40 consecutive days, 4 months (one day per week), or even 2 months (two days per week). Either way, you must be committed and consistent for lasting change.

Let's start releasing, and remember:

You are WORTH the CHANGE!

With love and purpose,
Dr. Theresa Pepcee' Edwards

Scan for an audio Introduction

Mental Toxins
Detox 1 - Detox 10

Emotionally Damaged   Detox 1 - Detox 5

Escalated Emotions   Detox 6 - Detox 9

Transitional: Feeling of Closure   Detox 10

DETOX 1

Awakening to Self

"When she feels invisible, do not judge her.
Nurture her. Love her. Help her."

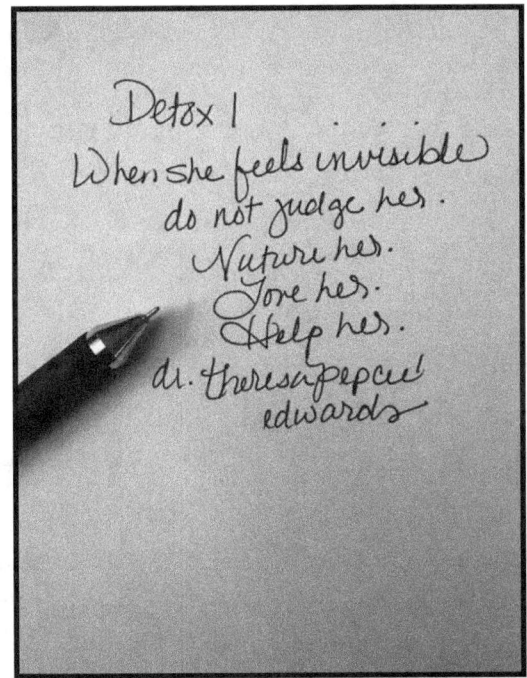

Detox 1

When she feels invisible
do not judge her.
Nurture her.
Love her.
Help her.

dr. theresa pepcue
edwards

Affirmation: Say this out loud, "I forgive myself. I am worth the change."

My Daily Reflection: "I looked in the mirror and saw her, but I was afraid to *see* her."

Personal Story:

A common question is, "When you look in the mirror, what do you see?" You see more than a reflection of yourself. You see every wound, all the scars, and everything you have encountered. Sometimes, you are so numb that you see nothing. Not even your reflection.

For years, I avoided mirrors. I never wanted to look at myself. It caused a great deal of anxiety. I did it only when it was absolutely necessary. I never liked what I saw. No matter what I did, I could not see myself. Through my detox, I learned why I felt this way.

I remember the day my dad was physically and verbally abusive to my mother. He was yelling, cursing, and saying terrible things. The house seemed so chaotic. My siblings were crying and confused. All while this was happening, my mother was trying to fix dinner. As my siblings and I entered the kitchen, my dad told my mother to get out. Then, he looked at me and said, "You get out, too, because you look like her." I was 8 years old.

At that time, we lived upstairs in a two-family flat with a closed back porch. We had a dog that slept in that space. We kept blankets for him to lay on. That night, this was where my mother and I slept. I can still remember the unpleasant smell of our dog and his blankets.

That evening was windy, rainy, and cold. My mother tried to keep me warm but how could she? I was still in my pajamas, and she only had the clothes she was wearing. Being a mother, I cannot imagine what she was feeling. I can barely remember how I felt. I do know, as I write about it, I am still overwhelmed with so many emotions.

From that day on, I resented looking like my mother and I absolutely hated my father.

Reflective Prompts:

Close your eyes. Breathe. Relax your mind. Be honest.

How do you feel about looking at yourself in the mirror? Do you have any fears? Do you like what you see?

_____

_____

_____

_____

_____

Your Daily Reflection:

What came up for you when you read today's reflection and my personal story? Write a sentence about your thoughts and feelings.

_____

_____

_____

_____

_____

Your Personal Story:

Write a short paragraph about your reflection. If you need more space, refer to your Companion Journal.

_____

_____

_____

_____

You Know Yourself:

What prescription would you write for yourself? What do you need to change, add, or remove to help you with negative thoughts or triggers?

_____

_____

_____

_____

_____

My Action:

My action from today's detox: I accepted how I felt about my mother and realized that it was because of the abuse that my father inflicted that caused me to feel bad about her. Over time, I learned that I did not resent my mother; she was a victim of domestic violence. I was a victim, as well. I hated my father for doing what he did to the both of us. Finally, in 2017, I began to be comfortable looking in the mirror. I told myself, "Hey, girl, I love you unconditionally. I need you every day." Also, at this time I appreciated looking like my beautiful mom.

Your Action:

1. Stand in front of the mirror and tell yourself what you like about yourself. Take your time. Initially, it may not be easy. *Breathe.* Now go for it. Look into your eyes and speak.

2. Find a word, quote, scripture, or mantra that you like and write it down. Place it where you can see it daily and when you need to, refer to it.

DETOX 2

A Million Pieces

"Transition to transpire a transformation."

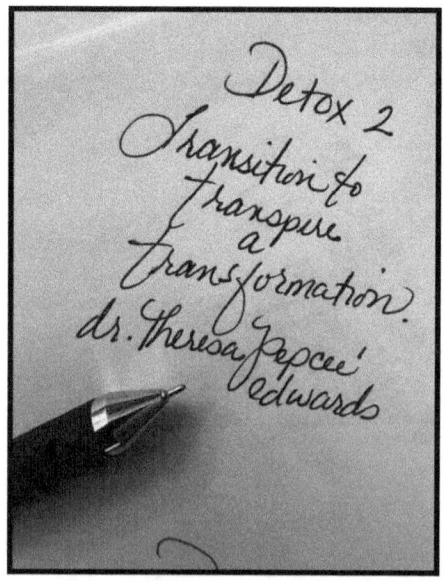

Affirmation: Say this out loud, "I forgive myself. I am worth the change."

My Daily Reflection: "My heart exploded into a million pieces."

Personal Story:

In 2008, I filed for divorce. It seemed that the divorce cracked the seal that kept my past in an invisible jar inside of me. In this jar, was all of my pain, the sexual abuse at 8 years old, the strained relationship with my mom, being homeless at 14, pregnant at 17 (abortion medically necessary), the abandonment of my firstborn's father who denied paternity, being shot in the leg in my early 20s, failed relationships, the loss of my first boyfriend, kidnapped and almost raped (age 14), my mom and step-dad dying 4 weeks apart (age 25), an intruder trying to break in while I was home (age 29), and now a divorce. I was in a dark place. There was no light to reach or work towards.

The jar shattered inside of me, and the contents started consuming my mind, heart, and thoughts. The radiating pain was stabbing me like sharp pieces of glass shards throughout my body. Although I purchased a notebook and pen and began to write, I recognized that I needed more help. I made a therapy appointment and took time off work.

While I awaited my therapy appointment, here's a poem that I wrote:

My Prayer (2008)

I lift my prayer up to You, Lord.
On the nights when I could not sleep.
On the days when I could not breathe.
You never left me.
I lift my prayer up to You, Lord.

While I lay there clutching my chest.
Wishing I could massage my heart.
You said, "I hear you, My child, this is a test."
Tomorrow is a brand-new start.

When I was alone—no love, no family, no friends, no one.
No one cared.
So much space around me.
I dropped to my knees; how could this be?
I add to my prayer, thank You for never deserting me.
Amen

Reflective Prompts:

Close your eyes. Breathe. Relax your mind. Be honest.

It is not easy when you think about things that have hurt you. Take a moment to think about the times you have exploded inside and could not breathe because of the painful memories. How did you cope with your emotions?

_____

_____

_____

_____

_____

Your Daily Reflection:

What came up for you when you read today's reflection and my personal story? Write a sentence about your thoughts and feelings.

_____

_____

_____

_____

_____

Your Personal Story:

Write a short paragraph about your reflection. If you need more space, refer to your Companion Journal.

_____

_____

_____

_____

_____

_____

You Know Yourself:

What prescription would you write for yourself? What do you need to change, add, or remove to help you with negative thoughts, or triggers?

_____

_____

_____

_____

_____

My Action:

My action today from the detox: To survive everything I went through, I had to fight first. Throughout it all, I realized that **I AM A FIGHTER**. I wrote the word "Fighter," posted it on my wall, and for the remainder of the detox journey, every day I repeated as my personal mantra, "I AM A FIGHTER."

Your Action:

1. Write one positive thing that you love about yourself. Post it so that you can see it every day.

2. Find a quote, scripture, or mantra that you like and write it down. Place it where you can see it and when you need to, refer to it.

DETOX 3

Am I Relevant?

"I let go of who I was to become who I am."

Affirmation: Say this out loud, "I forgive myself. I am worth the change."

My Daily Reflection: "I questioned why I was born."

Personal Story:

When I think about my childhood, I try to focus on the good times, but it is hard when you associate your childhood with pain. I have many memories of my father's abuse and until I started my 40-day journey and writing this book, I had blocked them out. For instance, he was always hard on me about my school grades. I remember that I was only allowed one S, which stood for Satisfactory, and the remaining grades had to be O's, which stood for Outstanding. Still, he would focus on the S. Once I moved to letter grades, I was allowed one B and the rest had to be A's. Anything outside of this requirement would warrant a severe punishment like the time I received two B's on my report card with the remaining grades, A's.

The punishment was unimaginable. He gave me licks on the back of my legs with a ruler. It was an extremely thick ruler that I believe he made. The licks were so hard that the impressions left deep marks. The back of my thighs were stinging badly and my skin had small, bloody openings. My pants would stick to the back of my thighs. I could not sit down and it was painful to walk. In school, I purposely got into trouble in order to stand in the corner.

As a result of his physical abuse, I remember always staying to myself and writing in notebooks or on pieces of paper. Pen and paper were my happiness. Writing helped me to process my daily feelings and express how I felt about what was happening to me. Honestly, I did not know that it was wrong; I thought that this was happening in other households as well. In fact, I never called what was happening to me abuse. I did not know it had a name. I viewed the instances as horrible punishments. Punishments that made you feel empty, confused, and disconnected. I felt like I should have never been born.

Reflective Prompts:

Close your eyes. Breathe. Relax your mind. Be honest.

Think about a time when you felt empty, confused, disconnected, or as a failure. Did you question your existence or your reason for being a part of this universe?

Your Daily Reflection:

What came up for you when you read today's reflection and my personal story? Write a sentence about your thoughts and feelings.

_____

_____

_____

_____

_____

Your Personal Story:

Write a short paragraph about your reflection. If you need more space, refer to your Companion Journal.

_____

_____

_____

_____

_____

You Know Yourself:

What prescription would you write for yourself? What do you need to change, add, or remove to help you with negative thoughts, or triggers?

_____

_____

_____

_____

_____

My Action:

My action from today's detox: I apologized to myself for questioning why I existed. I told myself, "I am so sorry that I wished that _you_ were never here." I began to understand that I had a purpose. I had a story of strength, courage, trials and tribulation, and through my FAITH, perseverance, and determination, I was able to change the narrative.

Your Action:

1. What would you apologize to yourself for? Take a moment to apologize to yourself. Tell yourself why you are apologizing. Show yourself understanding, kindness, and patience. Forgive yourself.

2. Find a quote, scripture, or mantra that you like and write it down. Place it where you can see it and when you need it, refer to it.

DETOX 4

Emptiness, 3rd grade.

"Sometimes you need to stand alone in your space,
to embrace your grace."

Affirmation: Say this out loud, "I forgive myself. I am worth the change."

My Daily Reflection: "Today, I realized my first encounter with feeling empty was when I was in 3rd grade."

Personal Story:

You feel happy, good, and amazing while blazing through life with no complaints but there is this part of you that has a sense of sadness. I recognized that I could be joyful and sad at the same time. As a child I was a loner; I did everything by myself. I remember 3rd grade so well because of the abuse I endured during that time.

While in 3rd grade, I was bullied by two girls in the neighborhood because they thought I was too smart. I did not defend myself because my father told me if I ever fought, I would regret it. This further pushed me into being in a space alone. This also taught me that I did not have a voice. So, I grew up not saying much about how I felt and would just go along to avoid conflict.

I never felt warm, experienced butterflies, excitement, or all the emotions that would make a person feel good inside. At a young age, I felt like my body was a shell with nothing inside. I was quiet, withdrawn, angry, and terrified of my father. My father did not allow me to cry. I had to take the pain and if I shed a tear or showed emotion, he would become angry.

This taught me not to feel. I was basically NUMB.

Reflective Prompts:

Close your eyes. Breathe. Relax your mind. Be honest.

Can you recall a time when you felt empty, hollow inside?

_____

_____

_____

_____

_____

Your Daily Reflection:

What came up for you when you read today's reflection and my personal story? Write a sentence about your thoughts and feelings.

_____

_____

_____

_____

_____

Your Personal Story:

Write a short paragraph about your reflection. If you need more space, refer to your Companion Journal.

_____

_____

_____

_____

_____

You Know Yourself:

What prescription would you write for yourself? What do you need to change, add, or remove to help you with negative thoughts, or triggers?

_____

_____

_____

_____

_____

My Action:

My action from today's detox: I told myself that I wanted to understand and feel my emotions. My past is a part of me but it can no longer define me. For years, if you did something to me, I would cut you off and would be okay never speaking to you again. I didn't understand why people would be upset until it happened to me. I felt horrible and vowed from that day, never to do it again. My take away from today is when I have an emotion, take time to process it and understand how it makes me feel. I have learned to treat others' emotions with delicacy, compassion, and respect as this is what I desire for myself.

Your Action:

1. The next time you have an emotion, take time to process and understand it. At that moment, tell yourself how you feel. Explain to yourself what you will do the next time that emotion surfaces.

2. Find a quote, scripture, or mantra that you like and write it
    down. Place it where you can see it and when you need it,
    refer to it.

DETOX 5

Rejection

"I am ENOUGH!"

Affirmation: Say this out loud, "I forgive myself. I am worth the change."

My Daily Reflection: "I dealt with so much rejection in my past relationships, and I did not realize how much damage had been done."

Personal Story:

Rejection… not accepted, not wanted, not needed. I did not always feel this but as I became older, these emotions became stronger. I often wondered how I would feel if I had not been violated. I carried that heaviness for a long time. I did not feel accepted by my mother. I suppose she did not know how to deal with me being sexually assaulted. She felt as if she did not protect me. But how could she? She was a victim too.

When I was 14 years old, we moved to the opposite side of town. I was scared because I barely knew anyone. According to my mom, we moved because she needed a fresh start on life. This is also when my mom put me out of the house. I was angry about my home life. I would challenge my mom when I felt as if she was not taking care of me and my siblings correctly. Looking back, I now understand that she was doing her best. After all, she was carrying her own pain and trauma.

I was too ashamed to call my family and tell them that I was homeless. No one knew. I would hang out with my friends and spend nights at their homes. I did this for as long as I could. I would alternate houses. I felt like a "throw away".

Rejection also showed up in my relationships or situations, things I perceived to be rejections but may not have been; however, this is how it felt. No matter what a person did, it did not seem to be enough because I longed for something that he could not provide. It took me years to figure out that what I longed for was already inside of me.

I felt invisible for nearly 27 years. Even when I was among people, I never felt connected. I am sure this feeling stemmed from my childhood as well. I remember being in college and while walking to class, wishing that I could be a giant, enabling me to step over all that I was feeling.

Reflective Prompts:

Close your eyes. Breathe. Relax your mind. Be honest.

When was the last time you felt rejected? Do you feel like you are enough? Are there certain people or situations that trigger the feeling of rejection?

Your Daily Reflection:

What came up for you when you read today's reflection and my personal story? Write a sentence about your thoughts and feelings.

_____

_____

_____

_____

_____

_____

_____

_____

Your Personal Story:

Write a short paragraph about your reflection. If you need more space, refer to your Companion Journal.

_____

_____

_____

_____

_____

You Know Yourself:

What prescription would you write for yourself? What do you need to change, add, or remove to help you with negative thoughts, or triggers?

_____

_____

_____

_____

_____

My Action:

My action from today's detox: I learned the source from which my determination and ability to persevere ignited. It was my resilience. Rejection was one of my most difficult emotions. It was deeply rooted. However, I am better and have a deeper understanding of what rejection means to me. Thinking back, I never gave up, regardless of how I was feeling. I kept believing that things would get better even if I could not see it.

Your Action:

1. Write a plan on how you will respond the next time you feel rejected. Be sure to add a step that will help you to process the rejection and help you to feel better afterwards.

2. Find a quote, scripture, or mantra that you like and write it down. Place it where you can see it and when you need it, refer to it.

DETOX 6

Feeling Uncomfortable

"One day you will love the inner you."

Affirmation: Say this out loud, "I forgive myself. I am worth the change."

My Daily Reflection: "Being uncomfortable made me feel ashamed and embarrassed."

Personal Story:

The first time I remember feeling uncomfortable was in the 4th grade. I was still processing the sexual assault. I did not fully understand what had happened to me. The night it happened, my mother was still missing. The day before, she said she was going to the store and would return shortly. I begged her to let me go with her but she said, "No, I will be back." I remember lying by the door, waiting for her to return. But she never did. A few weeks later, it was discovered that she had checked herself into the hospital to get help.

On the evening that I was molested, my father had returned home drunk. He called me to the table and pulled a 6 pack of Colt 45 out of a large paper bag. He laid a huge butcher knife in front of him. He gave me a can and told me to drink it. Then, he gave me the butcher knife and told me to push it into his side. I "faked" pushing because I did not want to do it. I pretended I was pushing hard by making faces and grunting sounds. He was so drunk that he did not realize I was faking. Luckily, the knife did not penetrate his skin.

On another occasion, after my mother left him, I went to see my grandmother and stayed the night. My grandmother lived downstairs from my father so I thought I would be safe. I was wrong. He had moved downstairs with his mother. That evening, he tried to put me in his bed, but my grandmother intervened and made him put me back in her bed. After that, I never saw my grandmother again. That was unfortunate because I was close to her. She died when I was in the 8th grade.

While sitting in my 4th-grade class, I would replay those nights over and over in my mind. I remember feeling trapped, disgusted, ashamed and embarrassed. I wanted to hide myself from everyone.

Reflective Prompts:

Close your eyes. Breathe. Relax your mind. Be honest.

Have you ever felt uncomfortable? What happened? Why did you feel this way?

Your Daily Reflection:

What came up for you when you read today's reflection and my personal story? Write a sentence about your thoughts and feelings.

_____

_____

_____

_____

_____

_____

Your Personal Story:

Write a short paragraph about your reflection. If you need more space, refer to your Companion Journal.

_____

_____

_____

_____

_____

You Know Yourself:

What prescription would you write for yourself? What do you need to change, add, or remove to help you with negative thoughts, or triggers?

_____

_____

_____

_____

_____

My Action:

My action from today's detox: This is where my self-image began. I never felt good because of what happened to me. I became ashamed of my body, as if I had done something wrong. I gained a significant amount of weight, as eating became my comfort. I did not like when someone made references to my body parts. This included cousins and their friends who would make jokes even though they were just being boys. I felt extremely uncomfortable each and every time.

Your Action:

1. Challenge any negative thoughts or emotions you may
    have as a result of feeling uncomfortable. For every nega-
    tive thought or emotion, replace it with a positive thought
    or emotion. Say to yourself, "I will no longer feel uncom-
    fortable."

2. Find a quote, scripture, or mantra that you like and write it
    down. Place it where you can see it and when you need it,
    refer to it.

DETOX 7

Admitting my Anger

"Freedom materializes when you acknowledge your truth."

Affirmation: Say this out loud, "I forgive myself. I am worth the change."

My Daily Reflection: "I can finally admit that I am ANGRY."

Personal Story:

For my entire life, I suppressed my childhood abuse and after my divorce, I suppressed that part of my life, too. I would tell myself, I am okay because it was a way to soothe my inner being. I never admitted to myself that I was extremely angry about the child-hood abuse and angry about my divorce, until today.

I am angry that my father verbally, physically, and sexually abused me. Who gave him the right? His abuse led me to use food as a comfort to hide *me* because I always felt uncomfortable.

I am angry that my marriage failed. I am angry that I felt massively rejected.

I am angry that I lied to myself all those years about how I really felt.

Reflective Prompts:

Close your eyes. Breathe. Relax your mind. Be honest.

Think about a situation that angered you but you told yourself, you were alright. Why do you think you suppressed your original emotion about the situation?

_____

_____

_____

_____

_____

Your Daily Reflection:

What came up for you when you read today's reflection and my personal story? Write a sentence about your thoughts and feelings.

_____

_____

_____

_____

_____

Your Personal Story:

Write a short paragraph about your reflection. If you need more space, refer to your Companion Journal.

_____

_____

_____

_____

_____

You Know Yourself:

What prescription would you write for yourself? What do you need to change, add, or remove to help you with negative thoughts, or triggers?

_____

_____

_____

_____

_____

My Action:

My action from today's detox: I learned from today's detox that suppressing hurtful experiences does not suppress the emotions. I took today to think about both experiences and explore why I was so angry. With my father, I felt violated and that he altered me. His abuse shaped how I viewed the world… especially males. With my marriage, I wanted it to work. You cannot recapture time; you can only keep moving. I am no longer held hostage in regard to how I really felt. I am free!

Your Action:

1. Travel through your mind and think about experiences that made or make you feel angry. Question yourself as to why you choose to suppress your true feelings. List the experiences, examine the situation, acknowledge how you really feel, forgive yourself for withholding your truth.

2. Find a quote, scripture, or mantra that you like and write it down. Place it where you can see it and when you need it, refer to it.

DETOX 8

Inwardly Crying

"Dry tears are just as painful as wet ones."

Affirmation: Say this out loud, "I forgive myself. I am worth the change."

My Daily Reflection: "I am crying, and I can't feel my tears. I can only feel them rolling down my face on the inside."

Personal Story:

My prayer one day was to be free from all the experiences that held me hostage in my mind, spirit, and soul. I felt empty and dry internally. I was consumed with the pain, the memories, and the challenge of trying to understand but not understanding. Crying, crying, crying, until one day I could not produce any more tears, externally.

I remember on several occasions, closing my eyes and feeling the tears stream down my cheeks. Even though I did not see my tears, the heaviness of my pain was still the same. I just wanted to know the "Why?"

Yes, the "Why." Why did it happen? Why is it happening? Why me? Why was the question with no answers… just circumstances, no rationale, just moments with no apologies. I kept trying to push myself to "get over it and move on." But this was only a temporary fix.

How did I get here? On the outside, I appeared to be together, quiet, approachable, mannerable, presentable, but on the inside my feelings were out of control.

This was the day I realized that I had become NUMB to life.

Reflective Prompts:

Close your eyes. Breathe. Relax your mind. Be honest.

Reflect on a time when you wanted to cry because you were in pain but you could not.

Your Daily Reflection:

What came up for you when you read today's reflection and my personal story? Write a sentence about your thoughts and feelings.

_____

_____

_____

_____

_____

Your Personal Story:

Write a short paragraph about your reflection. If you need more space, refer to your Companion Journal.

_____

_____

_____

_____

_____

You Know Yourself:

What prescription would you write for yourself? What do you need to change, add, or remove to help you with negative thoughts, or triggers?

_____

_____

_____

_____

_____

My Action:

My action from today's detox: I am not perfect. I realized that being angry would prompt me to lash out or take my anger out on someone else. I have learned to find healthy ways to address my anger such as writing or listening to music. I also learned that I may not ever understand my "why"; therefore, I have made amends with myself to accept that this is okay. And no matter how much I cry internally or externally, my life was and is not a mistake. I have a purpose.

Your Action:

1. Ask yourself, "When you feel angry, do you feel powerless? Why or why not? How do you respond to your anger? What are some ways you can express your anger in a healthy way?"

2. Find a quote, scripture, or mantra that you like and write it down. Place it where you can see it and when you need it, refer to it.

DETOX 9

Another Failed Relationship

"Fall in love with the one whose love is greater than your insecurities, your flaws, your pain, your wall."

Affirmation: Say this out loud, "I forgive myself. I am worth the change."

My Daily Reflection: "In most of my relationships I was told, "You are too emotional."

Personal Story:

The demise of my marriage was my biggest heartbreak. It felt as if my marriage was dissolving in my hands. It seemed like I was trying to keep the sand from running through my fingers. It did not matter how hard I clutched my hands together, the sand kept running out, until it was gone. This is how I felt about my marriage ending. No matter how hard I tried, it was still ending.

At times, out of nowhere, I would start to experience emotional exhaustion because my faith in LOVE had vanished. I could not pray for love anymore. I would sit and think about my relationships, trying to figure out what I could have done differently. I ended with the same thought,: "You did your best. It was not meant for you." But this did not make me feel better. It was a statement I told myself to get my mind through the moment. I still wanted to know WHY it was not.

As I engaged in other relationships, the common statement was, "You are too emotional." For a long time, I did not understand what this statement meant.

This journey helped me to realize that in my relationships, I was looking for my mate to be my ALL and that I would be his. It had nothing to do with me loving myself. It was about a big void in my heart and soul. I wanted to be in love and loved, wanted, and needed.

Reflective Prompts:

Close your eyes. Breathe. Relax your mind. Be honest.

Do you share your needs with your significant other and people in your life or do you keep it inside? Do you feel like your emotional needs are met? If not, why do you think your needs are unmet?

_____

_____

_____

_____

_____

Your Daily Reflection:

What came up for you when you read today's reflection and my personal story? Write a sentence about your thoughts and feelings.

_____

_____

_____

_____

_____

Your Personal Story:

Write a short paragraph about your reflection. If you need more space, refer to your Companion Journal.

_____

_____

_____

_____

You Know Yourself:

What prescription would you write for yourself? What do you need to change, add, or remove to help you with negative thoughts, or triggers?

_____

_____

_____

_____

_____

My Action:

My action from today's detox: I recorded myself speaking about what I need in a relationship; then, I played it back. The first time, the content of my message was confusing. I sounded nervous and uncertain about my needs. Then I decided to research my love language and write down what I desired.

I recorded myself again and this time, my content was clear. My voice was confident and I did a great job explaining to myself what I needed. This helped me to be able to articulate with assurance my needs to others.

Your Action:

1. Take a few minutes to think about what you need in a relationship. Next, without rehearsing, record yourself explaining your needs. Play it back. Examine if you were easily understood. This process will help you to become confident when expressing your needs to other people.

2. Find a quote, scripture, or mantra that you like and write it down. Place it where you can see it and when you need it, refer to it.

DETOX 10

Transitional: Feeling of Closure

"Closure quiets my inner soul."

Affirmation: "Closure quiets my inner soul."

Upon completion of Detox 1 - Detox 9, let's gather our thoughts, feelings, and emotions.

My Transitional Thoughts:

1. Reflection

My Detox 1 - Detox 9 summary:

As I sat and thought about Detox 1 - Detox 9, I found that I had a plethora of emotional baggage. Having open emotional items in my life are a hindrance to bringing balance to my overall emotional well-being.

Reflective Prompts:

What did I learn about mental toxins?

I needed to define what closure looks like in my life. Closure is accepting, embracing, and acknowledging the outcome but more importantly believing the truth.

2. Restorative Practices

- Affirmation Meditation:
  - Sit quietly and repeat the affirmation: "I AM WORTH THE CHANGE." Focus on each word and let it sink in.

Your Transitional Thoughts:

1. Reflection

Summarize your thoughts from Detox 1-9:

_____

_____

_____

_____

_____

Reflective Prompts:

What did you learn about your mental toxins?

_____

_____

_____

_____

_____

2. Restorative Practices

- Affirmation Meditation:
    - Sit quietly and repeat the affirmation: "I AM WORTH THE CHANGE." Focus on each word and let it sink in.

Preparing for the Next Phase: Healing

In the next phase, we'll focus on healing. Think about how healing can restore, rebuild, and rejuvenate your inner being.

- Action Step:
    - Think about how good it will feel to have a day free from past hurt and pain.

Scan for an audio Introduction

Healing
Detox 11 - Detox 19

DETOX 11

Dear Self: The Apology

"There is a thick layer between me and the world.
It is an unexplainable disconnection."

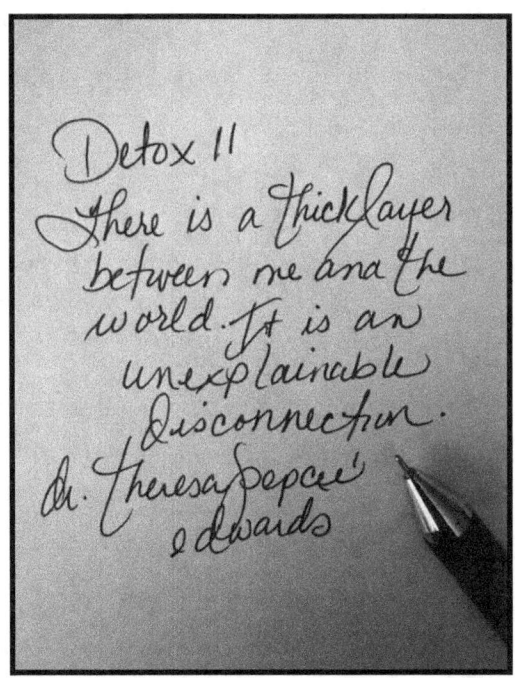

Affirmation: Say this out loud, "I forgive myself. I am worth the change."

My Daily Reflection: "I am sorry that it took me so long to apologize."

Personal Story:

I was thinking of a way to repair the relationship I had with myself. I needed to do this before I could repair relationships with other people in my life. After several hours of brainstorming, I decided to write an apology letter to myself. I needed to let myself know that I was sorry for taking so long to love and accept me. I did not realize how much I needed to respect my own feelings.

As I wrote my letter, I started to feel less heavy in my heart. I had emotional tension that kept me from enjoying what the world had to offer. I felt disconnected. This letter was the beginning of me reconnecting with myself. I experienced a soothing emotion that gave me the hope of a new beginning.

After I finished writing my letter, I also decided to list people that I owed an apology. My list included family and friends. It was difficult. The first individuals I apologized to were my children. My brokenness definitely impacted my parenting. I had to learn how to show love through affection and not things.

Reflective Prompts:

Close your eyes. Breathe. Relax your mind. Be honest.

Do you owe yourself an apology? Do you owe others an apology?

Your Daily Reflection:

What came up for you when you read today's reflection and my personal story? Write a sentence about your thoughts and feelings.

_____

_____

_____

_____

_____

Your Personal Story:

Write a short paragraph about your reflection. If you need more space, refer to your Companion Journal.

_____

_____

_____

_____

_____

You Know Yourself:

What prescription would you write for yourself? What do you need to change, add, or remove to help you with negative thoughts, or triggers?

_____

_____

_____

_____

_____

My Action:

My action from today's detox: Writing an apology letter to myself opened my eyes to how important it is to respect my feelings as I respect others. I need to trust myself to take care of me. This was a start, a new way of doing so.

Your Action:

1. Grab a good pen and a nice piece of paper, start with "Dear Self, I am sorry it took so long for me to apologize to you." Next, explain to yourself why you are apologizing and what you are apologizing for. Last, develop a list of who you would like to apologize to. You can keep the list or you can create an apology plan. It is up to you to decide.

2. Find a quote, scripture, or mantra that you like and write it down. Place it where you can see it and when you need it, refer to it.

DETOX 12

R²: Release & Relive

"Be free to live, again."

Affirmation: Say this out loud, "I forgive myself. I am worth the change."

My Daily Reflection: "I need my heart and emotion to be 100% pure."

Personal Story:

I realized that my heart was a holding space for emotions that I needed to let go. How can I become "whole" if I am holding on to "What ifs" and memories of things that hurt me? As I began acknowledging what I was holding on to, I started to feel different. It's strange because some parts of me wanted to hold on, just to feel like I had something, even if it did not make sense. Then, another part of me felt a sigh of relief, when I released the "what if" or the memory.

It took me some time to do this because some things I had held onto for a long time. These things gave me hope; at least, this is what I told myself. Early on in life, I fell in love with someone; we parted and never saw each other again. But, I would hold on to the thought of thinking HE was my one and that we would meet and fall in love again.

Reflective Prompts:

Close your eyes. Breathe. Relax your mind. Be honest.

Are you holding on to the "What Ifs"? Are you harboring memories that hurt you?

Your Daily Reflection:

What came up for you when you read today's reflection and my personal story? Write a sentence about your thoughts and feelings.

_____

_____

_____

_____

_____

Your Personal Story:

Write a short paragraph about your reflection. If you need more space, refer to your Companion Journal.

_____

_____

_____

_____

_____

You Know Yourself:

What prescription would you write for yourself? What do you need to change, add, or remove to help you with negative thoughts, or triggers?

_____

_____

_____

_____

_____

My Action:

My action from today's detox: I realized that I cannot hold things in my heart. To have a pure heart, it needs to be free, clear, open and not attached to old memories. I was dreaming of things to happen that may never have become a reality. Being free and clear also meant being detached physically and emotionally from individuals who do not reciprocate my feelings towards them.

Your Action:

1. Write down what having a pure heart means to you. Now do an inventory of your heart and access what you need to remove to reach your definition. Next, think about how this makes you feel.

2. Find a quote, scripture, or mantra that you like and write it down. Place it where you can see it and when you need it, you will be able to reference it.

DETOX 13

Get Unstuck

"PUSH until you MOVE."

Affirmation: Say this out loud, "I forgive myself. I am worth the change."

My Daily Reflection: "Sometimes, I feel mentally and physically paralyzed."

Personal Story:

Although I was feeling good and physically moving, at times, I felt stuck. The thought of uncertainty, the unknown, and lack of understanding would paralyze me. I would find myself trying to understand the 20 years I spent with one person and how the marriage failed. The anxiety of not knowing if I would meet someone to spend my life with scared me. Even though I was praying, trying to make good decisions on who I allowed in my life, I still felt STUCK at times.

I felt like I could accomplish anything I set my mind to but the one thing I could not control was who would love me—and that paralyzed me.

When I would feel stuck, it was because my mind would be overwhelmed with trying to figure out or understand the circumstance. I know that GOD has the answers and that HE will never leave my side. This was beyond my FAITH. This was about me needing answers.

Reflective Prompts:

Close your eyes. Breathe. Relax your mind. Be honest.

Have you ever felt stuck, unable to make decisions or confused?

Your Daily Reflection:

What came up for you when you read today's reflection and my personal story? Write a sentence about your thoughts and feelings.

_____

_____

_____

_____

_____

Your Personal Story:

Write a short paragraph about your reflection. If you need more space, refer to your Companion Journal.

_____

_____

_____

_____

_____

You Know Yourself:

What prescription would you write for yourself? What do you need to change, add, or remove to help you with negative thoughts, or triggers?

_____

_____

_____

_____

_____

My Action:

My action from today's detox: Feeling paralyzed would overwhelm me so I took time to accept that I will never understand things that have happened in my life. I also needed to be honest with myself about what I wanted to do in my life. Feeling stuck meant that I was not making prosperous moves, achieving, or progressing. I learned to *PUSH* through, *PERSEVERE* despite, and *PRESS* forward regardless to how I was feeling.

Your Action:

1. Write down things that make you feel stuck, paralyzed. Visualize how you would resolve the situation. Write a plan, if applicable, on how you could change the outcome of that situation. Last, write down two things you can do if you find yourself feeling stuck.

2. Find a quote, scripture, or mantra that you like and write it down. Place it where you can see it and when you need it, refer to it.

DETOX 14

Rejuvenation (Rejecting Rejection)

"Learn to love you. Appreciate your quiet thoughts.
Say sweet things to yourself."

Affirmation: Say this out loud, "I forgive myself. I am worth the change."

My Daily Reflection: "I refuse to let rejection destroy me."

Personal Story:

The moment I realized my life had purpose was the day I realized that rejection did not define me. Being rejected made me feel inadequate, giving me the feeling of not being enough. Even within my career, wanting a position or a specific salary and not being granted either, I would question my value.

Rejection from a relationship is piercing. At one point in my life, I dreaded leaving home to come back to the emptiness. It was hard. No one to do life with. Sometimes, you want to share your day, thoughts, or dreams with someone and to experience moments of togetherness, concern, and shared happiness.

I pushed myself to travel through my memories to identify why rejection created a dark space for me. Being rejected ignited an emotion that was indescribable. My journey revealed that I had never felt accepted.

It started with the sexual violation by my father and the strained relationship with my mother. Remembering that I was bullied in the 3rd grade challenged how I socialized in school. Failed relationships. Failed marriage. It all made sense.

Reflective Prompts:

Close your eyes. Breathe. Relax your mind. Be honest.

How do you feel about rejection? How do you handle rejection?

Your Daily Reflection:

What came up for you when you read today's reflection and my personal story? Write a sentence about your thoughts and feelings.

_____

_____

_____

_____

_____

Your Personal Story:

Write a short paragraph about your reflection. If you need more space, refer to your Companion Journal.

_____

_____

_____

_____

_____

You Know Yourself:

What prescription would you write for yourself? What do you need to change, add, or remove to help you with negative thoughts, or triggers?

_____

_____

_____

_____

_____

My Action:

My action from today's detox: I developed a plan for feeling rejected. First, I will accept the rejection. Second, I will reject the rejection. Third, I will tell myself, no matter how I am feeling that I love me. I am amazing. This was not in my plan. Fourth, I removed others' expectations from my life. I gave myself permission to live. I no longer surrendered my power to others to create my narrative. I am no longer a supporting character in my own life—I am the star, the main character, the director, and author. I am worthy!

Your Action:

1. Develop your rejection plan. Be specific. Be positive. More importantly, make sure it is doable. As you grow, you can revise your plan to fit where you are in your life. If you choose to share your plan, understand that everyone has an opinion and sometimes this can be more overwhelming than the plan itself.

2. Find a quote, scripture, or mantra that you like and write it down. Place it where you can see it and when you need it, you will be able to reference it.

DETOX 15

Unhealed = Unhealthy

"Take care of your emotions to have a greater outcome."

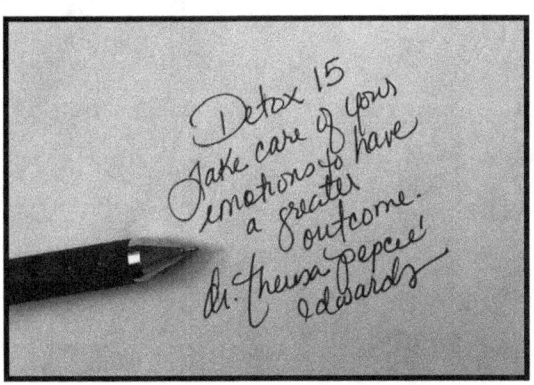

Affirmation: Say this out loud, "I forgive myself. I am worth the change."

My Daily Reflection: "I need to do better, to be better."

Personal Story:

Because I suppressed my feelings, my body became a holding cell for my emotions. My mind was always overloaded with thoughts and painful experiences. Basically, everything about me, whatever happened to me was held hostage within me. As I thought more about this, I realized that my entire body, my mind, my soul was infected with unresolved issues and unhealed wounds.

Is this why I have stomach issues, headaches periodically and unexplainable aches throughout my body? Is this why I have failed relationships or tend to entertain situations that are clearly not providing me with what I need? It was becoming clear to me that my unresolved emotions were creating detrimental situations. I told myself, I need to deal with these questions.

One thing I want to share is that my unresolved emotions led to me having weight issues. I was addicted to food. I became an emotional eater. This was a coping mechanism I used throughout my life. Whenever I would feel anxious, uncomfortable, sad, lonely, even happy, I would eat.

I needed help with my addiction. I was not afraid to admit that to myself. In 2017, I started the journey. My highest weight was 299 pounds. Today, I weigh 180 pounds. I make better food choices and I work out. But I was still having challenges with my health because of unresolved emotional issues.

As far as relationships, I will no longer love people who do not have the same amount of love for me. This is the most important thing I could have done for myself. The disappointment that comes with wanting something from someone who does not give it back is too harmful to my emotional well-being. It made me feel like I did not deserve to be loved.

I thought it was okay to accept a minimal dosage of love. Because of my childhood, I never required someone to love me fully. I accepted what was shared because I believed that some love was better than no love at all. After all, no love is what I had experienced most of my life.

Reflective Prompts:

Close your eyes. Breathe. Relax your mind. Be honest.

Do you have unresolved emotional issues? Are these unresolved emotions affecting your mental well-being or health? Do you need to seek help for an addiction?

Your Daily Reflection:

What came up for you when you read today's reflection and my personal story? Write a sentence about your thoughts and feelings.

_____

_____

_____

_____

_____

Your Personal Story:

Write a short paragraph about your reflection. If you need more space, refer to your Companion Journal.

_____

_____

_____

_____

_____

You Know Yourself:

What prescription would you write for yourself? What do you need to change, add, or remove to help you with negative thoughts, or triggers?

_____

_____

_____

_____

_____

My Action:

My action from today's detox: I had to change this and I did. I NOW put me first. I NOW check in with my emotions. I NOW exit when it is not what I need. I no longer prioritize people who do not extend the same. I am worthy of being loved and feel love to the fullest. I noticed as I evolved with my 40-day human detox, I started feeling better health wise, mentally, physically, and emotionally.

Your Action:

1. Decide what you need to change. Think about why you need to change it. Think of the benefit of the change. List the reasons for the change and how you will feel about the changes. Post it or save it to be able to read it as a reminder whenever you need to. If you have an addiction, contact resources for assistance.

2. Find a quote, scripture, or mantra that you like and write it down. Place it where you can see it and when you need it, refer to it.

DETOX 16

Hurting Heartbeat

"Take time to massage your heart.
Do what's needed to ease the pain."

Affirmation: Say this out loud, "I forgive myself. I am worth the change."

My Daily Reflection: "Despite it all, I have to learn to be my own joy and happiness."

Personal Story:

My heart is loveable yet lonely. The loneliness is not because I am away from people; it is due to the desire to have unconditional love and not feel abandoned. People always say to love yourself. The question is "What happens after that?" I still feel the same. I realized I needed more than just falling in love with myself, I needed to massage my heart.

Massaging my heart meant that I needed to process my hurt. Heart pain for me is a different pain that travels throughout my body. It is hard to describe because it is a persistent pain that occurs every time my heart would beat. With each thump, I would hold my chest, trying to breathe as gently as possible.

I started thinking of ways to massage my heart even though it was physically impossible. The first thing I did was decide what that meant; it meant that I wanted a sincere heart. A sincere heart that was not attached to individuals who were not emotionally attached to me. Second, that meant not being intertwined with anyone sexually who did not have my best interest at heart. Third, it meant removing myself from the space of those who inflicted harm towards me.

Reflective Prompts:

Close your eyes. Breathe. Relax your mind. Be honest.

How will you massage your heart? What does that look like for you?

Your Daily Reflection:

What came up for you when you read today's reflection and my personal story? Write a sentence about your thoughts and feelings.

_____

_____

_____

_____

_____

Your Personal Story:

Write a short paragraph about your reflection. If you need more space, refer to your Companion Journal.

_____

_____

_____

_____

_____

You Know Yourself:

What prescription would you write for yourself? What do you need to change, add, or remove to help you with negative thoughts, or triggers?

_____

_____

_____

_____

_____

My Action:

My action from today's detox: I needed balance. Finding balance within your heart can be challenging, especially if there is more than one emotion or if one emotion is dominating. I no longer wanted to be better and broken at the same time. I needed to be better at all times. Lastly, I told myself, "You cannot control other people's intentions. You are responsible for recognizing when their intent is not in alignment with you."

Your Action:

1. Write what massaging your heart will mean to you. Next, write 2 or more ways that you will massage your heart. Third, implement your plan.

2. Find a quote, scripture, or mantra that you like and write it down. Place it where you can see it and when you need it, you will be able to reference it.

DETOX 17

Selfish Self

"Courageously care for you."

Affirmation: Say this out loud, "I forgive myself. I am worth the change."

My Daily Reflection: "I am responsible for caring for myself."

Personal Story:

I am not a selfish person. It was hard for me to embrace this concept because it is not who I am. But I needed to do this. This one time, I needed to be concerned with myself exclusively. If this means detaching from the world for a brief moment, so be it.

When we decide to go on a vacation, we do a number of things to prepare for a successful trip. We plan, decide the number of days, select where we are going, how to get there, pay for the trip, purchase what's needed, pack what we need, make sure everyone is good, make sure the responsibilities for our jobs are taken care of and then we happily tell people.

People are excited for you. Here are a few responses we may receive: "have fun", "you deserve it", "take plenty of pictures" etc. We feel even better because these are all good things. But if I must add, going on vacation only temporarily pauses all the painful turmoil we have inside. Once we return, it's back to feeling the same.

So, I decided to go on a HUMAN vacation to help me gain some type of control over things that were happening in my life. To prepare, I selected where I wanted to go. I stayed at a local hotel with great amenities and with restaurants in the area. I decided to do a Friday - Sunday stay. I purchased or packed: relaxation clothes, notebooks, pens, highlighters, and white out.

I added a one-day preparation day to my HUMAN vacation. I had an undisturbed day at home. I listed all of my financial accounts (credit cards, banking, and loans). In addition, I listed all my bills for my home and business, along with any balances. I printed a copy of my resume. I felt it was always good to review and update; you never know when you will need it. I printed a copy of my personal, professional, and business goals. Lastly, I did a weekend agenda. This was my accountability tracker to make sure I stayed focused. On this agenda was relaxation time which included watching the television (I am a binge watcher), gym, swimming, etc.

Once I checked in, I removed all distractions which included communications. I only made a phone call to check on and check in. I took time to explore my emotions, embrace myself, look over every area of my life: finances, spirituality, relationships, career, family, my businesses, health, and love. When I returned home, I felt so rejuvenated, confident, and in control. I had a plan and that meant everything to me.

When I told people I was going on a HUMAN vacation, the responses were opposite. To my surprise, one response was, "what's wrong with you?", another one, "you acting funny". I further explained by sharing what I did to prepare and some of the responses were "really?", "that's good", "oh okay" and so forth. And the biggest one: "That is not a vacation. I am not paying for any hotel that's in my city."

Needless to say, this was interesting. We are cheered on to take a "personal vacation" but scrutinized for taking a "check on you" vacation.

Reflective Prompts:

Close your eyes. Breathe. Relax your mind. Be honest.

Are you unconditionally taking good care of yourself emotionally, physically, and financially?

Your Daily Reflection:

What came up for you when you read today's reflection and my personal story? Write a sentence about your thoughts and feelings.

_____

_____

_____

_____

_____

Your Personal Story:

Write a short paragraph about your reflection. If you need more space, refer to your Companion Journal.

_____

_____

_____

_____

_____

_____

_____

You Know Yourself:

What prescription would you write for yourself? What do you need to change, add, or remove to help you with negative thoughts, or triggers?

_____

_____

_____

_____

_____

My Action:

My action from today's detox: My well-being is attached to me. It is what guides me and keeps my outlook on life positive and healthy. It helps me make good decisions and thrive. When I feel overwhelmed and need to check in with every aspect of my life, I will unapologetically take a HUMAN vacation. I am committed to routinely taking a HUMAN vacation, 1 weekend, 3 times per year, April, August, and December.

Your Action:

1. Develop a HUMAN vacation plan. Determine how many times per year, decide the length of time for each, put it on your calendar, and set aside a budget. Examine every aspect of your life. Keep track of your process in a notebook or journal. At the end of the year celebrate your victories, review areas of concern, and be proud of yourself for being consistent.

2.   Find a quote, scripture, or mantra that you like and write it down. Place it where you can see it and when you need it, refer to it.

DETOX 18

Forgive Me

"I am not perfect in all areas of my life.
I will shine in the areas where I can."

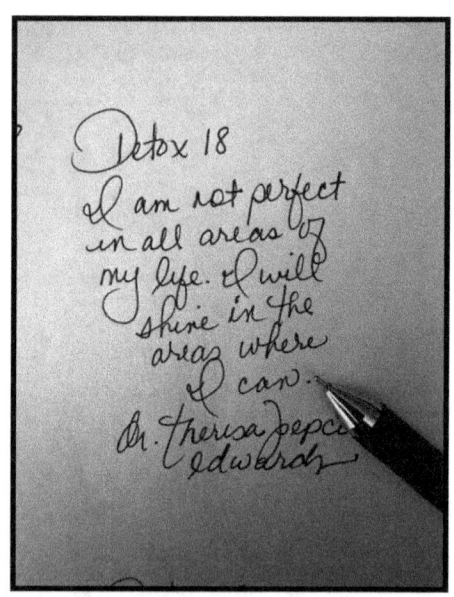

Affirmation: Say this out loud, "I forgive myself. I am worth the change."

My Daily Reflection: "I apologize for all that I have done to me."

Personal Story:

I apologize for not always doing things in the best interest of me. I apologize for not taking care of myself. I deserve to always have my undivided attention and to be treated with love, care, and sweetness. Self, I love you and I understand why prioritizing you is important.

Holding on to unhealthy thoughts and experiences allowed me to feel trapped in my own body. Holding on because I am afraid of being free… free from pain, rejections, emptiness, sadness, and the future. Sometimes, the fear of change and the unknown causes stress and anxiety. But I am ready for the new walk.

When I tell my story, I open up with "Let me apologize for the abuse you have endured. I am so sorry that you experienced the trauma that has happened to you. No, I am not the perpetrator, but I am someone who cares about you, who loves you, who wants to see you become free from being held hostage of any wrong doings. I say this to you because this is what I wanted to hear, needed to hear. What I am saying to you, I say to myself all the time." To the person reading my detox for today, I am sending the above message to you as well.

Another aspect of forgiving myself is to forgive others. I cannot honestly say that I have forgiven my father for what he did (sexual, physical, and verbal abuse). This will take some time, and it is okay! I do know that I am not holding on to it. As long as I continue to work on forgiveness, I will be moving closer to forgiving him. As of now, I have made peace, and this is where I am with it.

Reflective Prompts:

Close your eyes. Breathe. Relax your mind. Be honest.

Is there someone that you are having a hard time forgiving? Explore your reasons why? Do you think you will ever be able to forgive them?

Your Daily Reflection:

What came up for you when you read today's reflection and my personal story? Write a sentence about your thoughts and feelings.

_____

_____

_____

_____

_____

Your Personal Story:

Write a short paragraph about your reflection. If you need more space, refer to your Companion Journal.

_____

_____

_____

_____

_____

_____

You Know Yourself:

What prescription would you write for yourself? What do you need to change, add, or remove to help you with negative thoughts, or triggers?

_____

_____

_____

_____

_____

My Action:

My action from today's detox: Apologizing to myself made me feel cared for. I felt relieved and joyous because I was giving myself a second chance to do better. Oftentimes, I would seek validation or support from people. I am learning on this detox that I am my first point of contact for myself. I cannot look for others to give me what I need. All I have to do is start the process and God will always send me what I need.

Your Action:

1. Write an apology letter to yourself. Be authentic and genuine. Write what you would like to hear someone say to you; write what you need.

2. Find a quote, scripture, or mantra that you like and write it down. Place it where you can see it and when you need it, you will be able to reference it.

TRANSITIONAL: DETOX 19

Peace, Perseverance, and Prayer

"It's okay to be in the 'ME, MYSELF & I' mode."

Affirmation: "It's okay to be in the "ME, MYSELF & I" mode.

Upon completion of Detox 11 - Detox 18, let's gather our thoughts, feelings, and emotions.

My Transitional Thoughts:

1. Reflection

My Detox 11 - Detox 18 summary:

Detox 11 - Detox 18 showed me I must always love me, love all the parts of me, love my flaws, my strengths and weaknesses. Loving me deeper than before will bring peace, comfort, and a sense of direction. Love is putting me first and giving myself what I need.

Reflective Prompts:

What did I learn about healing?

Healing is about working through the pain and being kind to myself along the way. I must always put God first and pray even when I feel like I do not have the strength.

2. Restorative Practices

- **Affirmation Meditation:**
  - Sit quietly and repeat the affirmation: "I AM AT PEACE. I WILL BE FREE. THE UNIVERSE GOT ME." Focus on each word and let it sink in.

Your Transitional Thoughts:

1. Reflection

Summarize your thoughts from Detox 11 - Detox 18:

_____

_____

_____

_____

_____

Reflective Prompts:

What did you learn about healing?

_____

_____

_____

_____

2. Restorative Practices

• Affirmation Meditation:

   ◦ Sit quietly and repeat the affirmation: "I AM AT PEACE. I WILL BE FREE. THE UNIVERSE GOT ME." Focus on each word and let it sink in.

Preparing for the Next Phase: Inner Peace

In the next phase, we'll focus on inner peace. Think about how it will feel to have an inner being that is calm and content.

• Action Step:

   ◦ Think about how it will feel to have inner peace. What emotions do you feel?

Scan QR Code for an audio introduction.

Inner Peace
Detox 20 - Detox 28

DETOX 20

Standing Still

"Guided. Grounded. Focused."

Affirmation: Say this out loud, "I forgive myself. I am worth the change."

My Daily Reflection: "Today I will step outside myself, to see myself."

Personal Story:

As a result of the abuse I endured, I struggled with keeping my mind from feeling out of control. I feared my father and he made me nervous because I never knew what was going to happen. This is when overwhelming thoughts would appear.

Today, I envisioned myself stepping outside of me and I was overwhelmed with what I witnessed. I saw a woman who could not be still, not physically but mentally. You could see that I was full of thoughts and emotions as if I was running this race with no specific destination. I was lost.

In my personal, professional, and even in my entrepreneurial world, I felt like I was all over the place. Sometimes, you can be doing so much and not accomplishing anything. I needed direction, instructions, or some type of guidance.

I needed to be absolutely still, quiet my mind, tell myself in the softest voice to "shhhh". Close my eyes and activate my listening skills. I prayed: "God, please guide me, ground me, and help me to become more focused. Help me to calm my thoughts, cease all movement in my mind. I want to hear from You. I need You. Amen"

Reflective Prompts:

Close your eyes. Breathe. Relax your mind. Be honest.

When was the last time you ceased all movement, not just physically but mentally? How did you feel?

Your Daily Reflection:

What came up for you when you read today's reflection and my personal story? Write a sentence about your thoughts and feelings.

_____

_____

_____

_____

_____

Your Personal Story:

Write a short paragraph about your reflection. If you need more space, refer to your Companion Journal.

_____

_____

_____

_____

_____

_____

_____

_____

You Know Yourself:

What prescription would you write for yourself? What do you need to change, add, or remove to help you with negative thoughts, or triggers?

_____

_____

_____

_____

_____

_____

_____

My Action:

My action from today's detox: I appreciated calming my mind so that I could hear what the universe is saying to me. At times, this is difficult for me to do. However, with consistency I will become better and more comfortable with being still.

Your Action:

1. Find a quiet space. Make it comfortable. Close your eyes. Breathe. Tell yourself in a soft nurturing voice, "Shhhhh." Ask the universe to guide you. Open your mind and activate your Listening skills. Enjoy no movement physically or mentally.

2. Find a quote, scripture, or mantra that you like and write it down. Place it where you can see it and when you need it, you will be able to reference it.

DETOX 21

The Gift of Awareness

"The greatest gift I can give myself is to know me."

Affirmation: Say this out loud, "I forgive myself. I am worth the change."

My Daily Reflection: "*Me*: Self *Self*: Yes *Me*: Do I know you? *Self*: Do you?"

Personal Story:

Today my mind and thoughts are calmer. I can take time to reflect, really think about who I am, who I desire to be, what about me makes me "ME". Seems like every time a relationship does not work out, I spend too much time trying to figure out the "WHY?" or when I was cheated on. I started questioning who I was. Why was I not enough?

I realized before I could question if I was enough, I needed to know who I was. Why do I think and act the way I do? What are my strengths… my weaknesses? What do I need? How do I feel? etc. I cannot believe, as basic as these questions are, I could not answer them.

I told myself, "You cannot answer the questions because you do not know who you are." OMG, how can I set goals and achieve them and not know who I really am. I was drowning in pain for so long that I never took time to learn about myself, or to try to understand me.

I needed to understand how I show up and respond to certain situations. Why is it easy for me to stop talking to people? Is it because I do not want to be hurt? Is it comfortable and safe? Or is it because I can avoid dealing with the situation and how I feel? Maybe, it's all four. I do not know.

This is what I need to explore. Today revealed the importance of being aware of how I think, respond to situations, my feelings, and what I stand for. Also, understanding what I say or do has an effect on people and myself.

Reflective Prompts:

Close your eyes. Breathe. Relax your mind. Be honest.

Are you ready for your self-discovery journey? Do you understand your beliefs, morals, and values? And why do you believe them? Are you aware of your emotions and how they impact individuals?

Your Daily Reflection:

What came up for you when you read today's reflection and my personal story? Write a sentence about your thoughts and feelings.

_____

_____

_____

_____

Your Personal Story:

Write a short paragraph about your reflection. If you need more space, refer to your Companion Journal.

_____

_____

_____

_____

_____

You Know Yourself:

What prescription would you write for yourself? What do you need to change, add, or remove to help you with negative thoughts, or triggers?

_____

_____

_____

_____

_____

My Action:

My action from today's detox: Today's detox really helped me dig deep into myself, push past the pain to get to my core. My life was complicated, it was like pulling all the thread off the spool to reach the beginning piece of the thread. I needed to start at the beginning to truly understand myself. The more aware I am of myself, the more I will grow, the more confident I will be, and most of all the more love I will give to myself.

Your Action:

1. This is a first step to becoming self-aware. Grab a sheet of paper and a pen. Answer these questions: (1) Do I understand what I need? (2) What do I need? (3) Do I understand my emotions? (4) Do I understand other people's emotions? (5) Am I aware of how I respond to situations? (6) Do I know what my beliefs and values are? Now you may develop 4 more questions that you would like to learn about yourself. This is an ongoing process. The more questions you ask your-

self, the more you will learn about who you are. Go as deep as you can.

2. Find a quote, scripture, or mantra that you like and write it down. Place it where you can see it and when you need it, refer to it.

DETOX 22

over, Over, OVER

"You move differently when you let go."

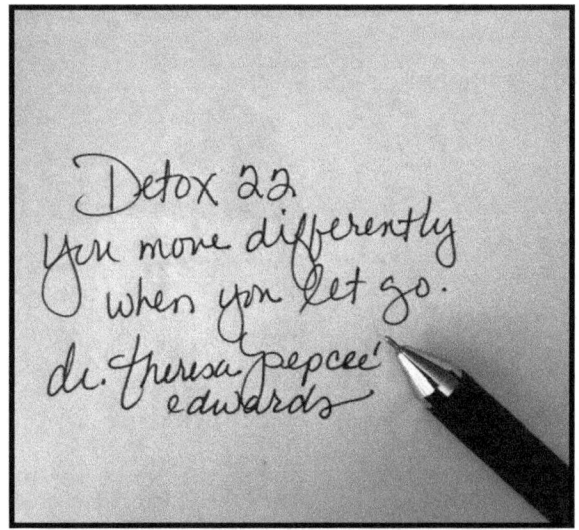

Affirmation: Say this out loud, "I forgive myself. I am worth the change."

My Daily Reflection: "I let go in order to grow."

Personal Story:

When I am stuck on something, I replay various versions in my mind. Overthinking and overanalyzing until I feel emotionally overwhelmed about the situation. I noticed that I overthink when I am uncertain about the decision, when I am upset about something or the unannounced pain that started me on this detox.

Overthinking and overanalyzing can trigger certain emotions. Depending on the circumstances, I can feel anxious, sad, angry and so forth. Sometimes, I can think negatively about the situation which turns into repeated negative thoughts. In other instances, I can be overthinking or overanalyzing about changing careers which triggers a panic attack or anxiety. I need to change my approach to how I mentally process things.

I noticed when my mind is not clear, I tend to make decisions based on emotions and this may not generate the best outcomes. In relationships, this may be seen as saying something hurtful or in a negative way. Then, I think about it and try to fix it.

Spending too much time pondering over things impacts my mental well-being. I said to myself, "Girl, let it go." whatever it is... "Let it go!"

Reflective Prompts:

Close your eyes. Breathe. Relax your mind. Be honest.

This is a jumpstart to understanding your thought process. What are your overthinking triggers? How does your overthinking affect your emotions?

Your Daily Reflection:

What came up for you when you read today's reflection and my personal story? Write a sentence about your thoughts and feelings.

_____

_____

_____

_____

_____

Your Personal Story:

Write a short paragraph about your reflection. If you need more space, refer to your Companion Journal.

_____

_____

_____

_____

_____

_____

_____

_____

You Know Yourself:

What prescription would you write for yourself? What do you need to change, add, or remove to help you with negative thoughts, or triggers?

_____

_____

_____

_____

_____

_____

_____

My Action:

My action from today's detox: I recognized that I needed a plan to maintain my mental well-being. I desire to be an authentic, good decision-maker who is in control of my thoughts and emotions. Each time, I will take a moment to learn the root cause. My goal is to become more self-aware.

Your Action:

1. Create your self-talk dialogue. Be aware when you are over-thinking and overanalyzing. Explore your thoughts and emotions. Talk to yourself. Use your internal or external voice. Encourage and inspire yourself. Be confident, bold, and speak with authority. If you are a visual person, dream, dream, dream. Dream about what makes you feel good. Guide the image until you are smiling, feeling empowered, and in control.

2. Find a quote, scripture, or mantra that you like and write it down. Place it where you can see it and when you need it, refer to it.

DETOX 23

Requesting your Presence

"Appreciating the 'NOW' is priceless."

Affirmation: Say this out loud, "I forgive myself. I am worth the change."

My Daily Reflection: "My thoughts are not still. I am always thinking."

Personal Story:

Living in the NOW is what I am struggling with. Being present to appreciate what is currently happening is a challenge for me. I have to tell myself that I am not concerned with what happened yesterday or what's going to transpire tomorrow. I am trying really hard not to focus on what took place in the past or what will manifest in the future.

I have built my life around staying ahead to keep from failing or becoming homeless again. I am always thinking about tomorrow and my future. Why am I struggling with this concept? Is it because I have spent my past and present intertwined?

To help me request my presence, I remembered this poem that I had written:

Dear God, YOU are AMAZING!

You HELD me through the abuse (sexual, physical, and verbal).

You HELD me when I was homeless at age 14.

You HELD me through my divorce.

You HELD me through my parenting.

You TOLD me to be strong and tell my story.

You TOLD me I was chosen to be a living witness.

You TOLD me YOU and only YOU can heal.

You TOLD me to have FAITH and you will CHANGE my heart from despair to deliverance.

I THANK YOU for my journey and for allowing it to be a testimony for others.

I THANK YOU for what YOU are doing in my life.

I THANK YOU for giving me the gift to inspire, educate, and motivate the inner being of others.

You HELD, You TOLD, I THANK YOU!

Amen

March 19, 2010 Revised: December 8, 2011

Remembering this poem was a start to helping me embrace the NOW. Reading today's detox helped me to see that I do not have to worry about my past or allow my future to become an obsession.

Reflective Prompts:

Close your eyes. Breathe. Relax your mind. Be honest.

Are you present? If not, how do you request your presence? If you are, how do you ensure that you are 100% present?

Your Daily Reflection:

What came up for you when you read today's reflection and my personal story? Write a sentence about your thoughts and feelings.

_____

_____

_____

_____

_____

Your Personal Story:

Write a short paragraph about your reflection. If you need more space, refer to your Companion Journal.

_____

_____

_____

_____

_____

_____

_____

_____

You Know Yourself:

What prescription would you write for yourself? What do you need to change, add, or remove to help you with negative thoughts, or triggers?

_____

_____

_____

_____

_____

_____

_____

My Action:

My action from today's detox: I can do this in small steps. Start by being grateful for the day, taking a moment to embrace where I am. Allow my mind to relax, to become free and clear of thoughts. I have to practice focusing on what is actually occurring in real time. Most importantly, I have to be consistent.

Your Action:

1. What does living in the NOW look like for you? Write down 2 or more ways that will help you live in the NOW. How often will you incorporate what you have written in your life?

2. Find a quote, scripture, or mantra that you like and write it down. Place it where you can see it and when you need it, you will be able to reference it.

DETOX 24

Declutter

"My mind is not a space for hurtful storage."

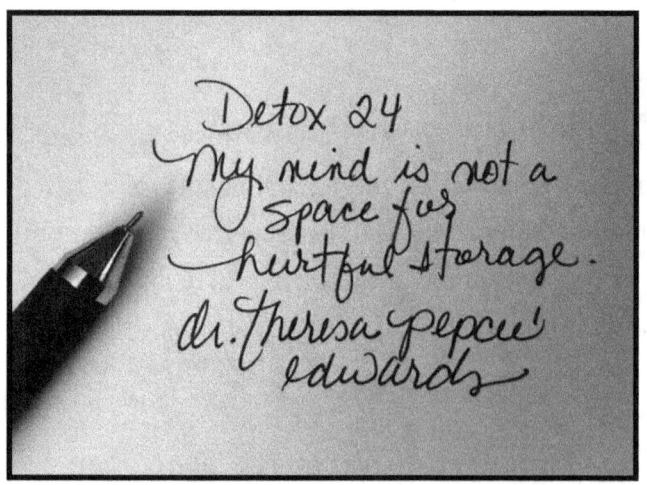

Affirmation: Say this out loud, "I forgive myself. I am worth the change."

My Daily Reflection: "I cannot think, eat, or sleep."

Personal Story:

The day I figured out that my mind was one big file cabinet with drawers, was the day that I started on a journey to organize my mind. I was so good at suppressing my emotions that when something happened, I stored the emotions in my mind. I did not try to deal with it, in fact I was not even concerned.

When I divorced my ex-husband, the pain was heavy; it felt like death. I was so alone, lonely, and withdrawn. I was alone at that time and was afraid of that feeling. To deal with it, I pushed it in several drawers… spaces within my mind. My mind was already on overload from my childhood, but I suppressed it anyway. My mind was also cluttered with financial challenges, my car and home needed repairs, and my children were hurting from the divorce. My youngest was newly diagnosed with asthma.

The day my mind and heart exploded, GOD guided me to a new beginning. One extremely cold day in January, I came home and the furnace stopped working. I looked into my almost 3-year-old's eyes and slid down the wall. I did not want her to see me break down. But she looked at me, as she sat on a small bead container with her bible and highlighter. She said, "Mom, GOD sent me here to take care of you." I looked at her with amazement and confusion. She said, "He is right here," as she looked behind herself. I looked too! She said, "He told me I am in the front and HE is in the back." I did not question it.

I stood up, thanked HIM and did what I did best. I grabbed a piece of paper and started writing everything that was on my mind. I assessed the pain in my heart, listed what I needed to do and executed a plan to rebuild my self-esteem and life.

Reflective Prompts:

Close your eyes. Breathe. Relax your mind. Be honest.

Is your mind overloaded? Do you have unresolved memories? Is your heart full of pain? Do you need closure?

Your Daily Reflection:

What came up for you when you read today's reflection and my personal story? Write a sentence about your thoughts and feelings.

_____

_____

_____

_____

_____

Your Personal Story:

Write a short paragraph about your reflection. If you need more space, refer to your Companion Journal.

_____

_____

_____

_____

_____

_____

You Know Yourself:

What prescription would you write for yourself? What do you need to change, add, or remove to help you with negative thoughts, or triggers?

_____

_____

_____

_____

_____

_____

_____

My Action:

My action from today's detox: I self-examined what was on my mind and categorized my thoughts. To rebuild my self-esteem, I decided to push myself outside of my comfort zone. I wanted to see myself in a new light. Organizing my mind, exploring my heart, and revitalizing my soul all contributed to helping me gain control of my thoughts, gave me the courage to remove things from my mind, and the strength to keep pushing.

I also did a "_Treat ME Day._" This day consisted of shopping for colors and clothes that I normally would not wear. I allowed the Sales Representative to pick out my outfits. Next, I saw a make-up artist. I had never seen myself with a full face of make-up. Lastly, I attended a photoshoot with the clothes I purchased. And what really made this day special was my friend driving me around as my personal chauffeur.

*The picture included in Detox 23 is a photo from the photoshoot.

At the photoshoot, I had a meltdown in the changing room. I was struggling with wearing the color yellow. It was brighter than any color I had ever worn. I had to keep reminding myself of the purpose of this experience. Before I knew it, I was crying and feeling overwhelmed. I started to hyperventilate.

My friend knocked on the door and asked, "T, are you ready?" I replied, "Yes". But I was not ready. I was ashamed and feeling uncomfortable. I was 37 and this is how I felt. Finally, I told myself, "your shirt is the color black." I decided that I was going to tell myself this statement throughout the photoshoot.

As I sat for the photoshoot, the photographer was preparing his camera. I sat down, took a deep breath, closed my eyes, started praying for God to help get through this difficult moment, and told myself, "You have on black." The photographer looked up and he said, "Pepcee' do not move. Stay… just as you are."

When I saw the picture, I cried because it spoke to me. I saw myself for the first time. I saw a woman who displayed a facial expression of calmness and relaxation. I also recognized that it was the beginning of finding a way to be comfortable with being seen. The color yellow was not bad looking on me. From that day forward, I have clothes with color in my wardrobe, including white! Ahhhh… life is so much better with a little color.

Your Action:

1. *Treat ME Day*: Book a photoshoot or have someone take your photos. Let someone else dress you! You cannot wear

colors that you would generally wear. Book a make-up artist. Let your friend drive you to the photoshoot. Sit in the back and enjoy the view. Breathe, say sweet things to yourself. Even if you are not comfortable with what you are wearing, push yourself to embrace the difficult and open your mind to seeing yourself in a new light.

2. Find a quote, scripture, or mantra that you like and write it down. Place it where you can see it and when you need it, refer to it.

DETOX 25

The Weight of Worry

"No more anchors on my ankles."

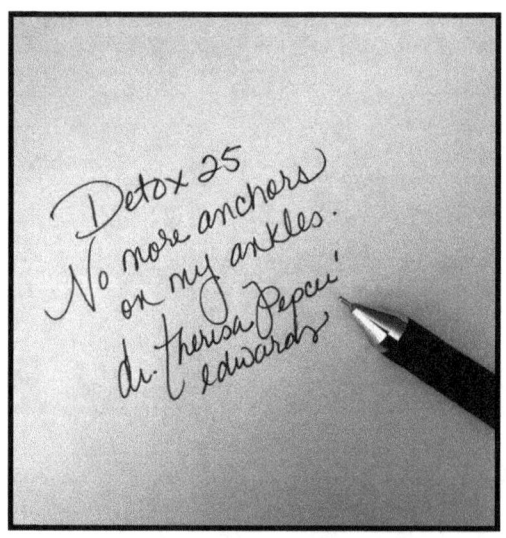

Affirmation: Say this out loud, "I forgive myself. I am worth the change."

My Daily Reflection: "The weight of my world is weighing me down."

Personal Story:

The fight to rebuild and restore what was taken from me weighed heavily on heart, mind, and soul. My ability to feel love, security, and protection was destroyed at one point in my life. As a result of this, I always felt as if I had anchors on my ankles holding me down. Taking a step forward seemed difficult. No matter how much I pushed, I could not step towards anything.

Why do I feel heavy? I started thinking about all the abuse and trauma I felt as a child and the one thing that broke me was being molested. I felt robbed. He took away my first experience. He violated my intimacy. No matter how hard I tried, I was never able to make that space whole.

Throughout my life, I felt numb when it came to sharing myself with someone along with all the emotions associated with it. When I turned 21, I confronted my father. Of course, he did not remember but I was strong enough to talk about every detail. I made him listen. I also asked him questions about his childhood because I desperately needed to understand his actions. He did share his view point and experiences of his childhood. It all made sense to me. This was also the first step towards some type of understanding and closure.

As I work through this detox, I am feeling lighter. I am learning new ways to restore and rebuild what has been broken. I am regaining and nurturing areas that need healing, and making revisions.

I am rejuvenating that part of me that was carelessly disrespected because of someone else's lack of consideration regarding me.

Reflective Prompts:

Close your eyes. Breathe. Relax your mind. Be honest.

Are there things in your life that are weighing you down? Do you always feel heavy and exhausted from it?

Your Daily Reflection:

What came up for you when you read today's reflection and my personal story? Write a sentence about your thoughts and feelings.

_____

_____

_____

_____

_____

Your Personal Story:

Write a short paragraph about your reflection. If you need more space, refer to your Companion Journal.

_____

_____

_____

_____

_____

You Know Yourself:

What prescription would you write for yourself? What do you need to change, add, or remove to help you with negative thoughts, or triggers?

_____

_____

_____

_____

_____

My Action:

My action from today's detox: For the first time, I wrote a letter to my father and I expressed how I felt. Afterwards, I shredded the letter. I felt relieved and at peace. I am working on not being angry about the situation.

Your Action:

1. Think about how you will release the weight that's weighing on you in your life? Write 1-2 strategies on how you will release that weight. You can write a letter, do a balloon release, write a book etc.

2. Find a quote, scripture, or mantra that you like and write it down. Place it where you can see it and when you need it, refer to it.

DETOX 26

Patience

"Breathe. Observe. Assess. Respond."

Affirmation: Say this out loud, "I forgive myself. I am worth the change."

My Daily Reflection: "I need to work on my patience."

Personal Story:

Overall I feel like I am a patient person. For today's detox, I wanted to examine when I struggle with patience. I cannot recall if I have ever taken the time to do this.

In my early twenties, I can remember being in college working on my associate degree. I had 4 classes and a lab. It was my second semester and I did not want to fail. Also, during this time, I had two small children. I remember sitting at the table with my material open in front of me with one child laying across my lap and the other one in my arms. I was quite frustrated, stressed, and overwhelmed. The emotions from this situation triggered how I was treated by my father. He was short tempered and would respond with violence.

From that day, I took time to learn how to plan to complete my task. I became a master of schedules. I would plan my day by listing what I needed to do, including running errands, etc. Every minute and second of the day was accounted for. Doing this assisted me with gaining control of my situation which helped me to learn patience.

To help myself strengthen my patience, I listed things that affect my ability to exercise it. Then I explored why this was an issue for me. To my surprise, I was shocked at what I did and did not have patience for. I had patience and tolerance for getting lost, losing my keys, completing several tasks and so forth. What I did not have patience for was procrastination, drama, and chaos.

Reflective Prompts:

Close your eyes. Breathe. Relax your mind. Be honest.

Think about what triggers your patience. Why is this a trigger for you? How do you handle the situation and/or person?

Your Daily Reflection:

What came up for you when you read today's reflection and my personal story? Write a sentence about your thoughts and feelings.

_____

_____

_____

_____

_____

Your Personal Story:

Write a short paragraph about your reflection. If you need more space, refer to your Companion Journal.

_____

_____

_____

_____

_____

You Know Yourself:

What prescription would you write for yourself? What do you need to change, add, or remove to help you with negative thoughts, or triggers?

_____

_____

_____

_____

_____

My Action:

My action from today's detox: I want to improve how I respond to individuals who procrastinate. Today's detox taught me that it's not up to me to determine how fast someone should respond to a situation that is affecting them. To help me, I listed 5 things I could do when I felt myself becoming annoyed: (1) Do not interrupt when the person is speaking (2) Remain calm and open (3) Breathe and count, if necessary (4) Understand that procrastination is okay (5) Accept people for who they are as it relates to procrastination. Improving my patience will have so many benefits including ensuring my emotional well-being is always in a healthy state.

Your Action:

1. What is your plan to improve your patience? List 2-5 strategies to help support you. Think about how to incorporate these strategies into your life.

2.   Find a quote, scripture, or mantra that you like and write it down. Place it where you can see it and when you need it, you will be able to reference it.

DETOX 27

Motivating Me

"Allergic to poverty. Addicted to success."

Affirmation: Say this out loud, "I forgive myself. I am worth the change."

My Daily Reflection: "If I am not moving, I am not progressing."

Personal Story:

I am a person of perseverance. My life has been filled with challenges, but I refused to let them define me. Although I dropped out of high school, I earned my GED and went on to accomplish what many thought was impossible. I earned my associate degree in two years, then completed both my bachelor's and master's degrees in another two years. In 2017, I earned a doctoral degree. I knew I had it in me, even when others doubted me—when they treated me like I was nothing and no one.

There was a time when I felt overlooked, invisible, and doubted by people. But I decided to lead with my actions, showing resilience, courage, and determination in the face of adversity. Even as a single parent on welfare with two children, I had to keep going. No matter what happened. I was determined to make it. I needed to plant a small seed of motivation within myself.

I promised myself that I would always keep going, no matter what was going on. When I was shot in my leg, after being released from the hospital, I went to school the next day. When I did not have a car, I did not allow it to hinder me. Here is what my Tuesday and Thursday looked like for the semester: 6 am: caught the bus to take my children to daycare, then took another bus to school for my morning class. 12 noon: took the bus to pick up the children from daycare. 2 pm - 4 pm: Feed and walk them to the sitter. 5:30

pm: Took the bus for my night class. 10 pm: Took a cab to pick up my children. I knew then, I had an appetite for success. I needed to remind myself to stay motivated.

Whenever I was faced with a setback, I told myself, "This isn't the end; it's just a step." Success is only one step away, so take it. You can be this way, too. You have the strength within you to persevere and keep going when life feels impossible. Reflect on what's in your heart and your determination to succeed, and remind yourself that no matter what, you have the power to rise above it all. If I can do it, you can, too!

Reflective Prompts:

Close your eyes. Breathe. Relax your mind. Be honest.

Do you struggle with motivation? Think about why you struggle.

Your Daily Reflection:

What came up for you when you read today's reflection and my personal story? Write a sentence about your thoughts and feelings.

_____

_____

_____

_____

_____

Your Personal Story:

Write a short paragraph about your reflection. If you need more space, refer to your Companion Journal.

_____

_____

_____

_____

_____

_____

_____

You Know Yourself:

What prescription would you write for yourself? What do you need to change, add, or remove to help you with negative thoughts, or triggers?

_____

_____

_____

_____

_____

_____

My Action:

My action from today's detox: I have an appetite to succeed. I am also determined. I keep going until my goal is accomplished. To help keep me motivated, I created a motivation day. I gave it the name of MOVE IT MONDAY. Every Monday I say this quote, "I am allergic to poverty. I am addicted to success." This jumpstarts my week and keeps me encouraged.

Your Action:

1. List what motivates you? Is it quotes, spiritual readings, watching motivational videos, etc.? Think about why these things motivate you. First, create your motivation day. Be creative, name it whatever you like or you can use what it is already known for. For example, Mondays are known as Motivational Mondays. Second, define what your success looks like. Remember, as you evolve, you may need to revise your trajectory towards success.

2. Find a quote, scripture, or mantra that you like and write it down. Place it where you can see it and when you need it, you will be able to reference it.

TRANSITIONAL: DETOX 28

Being Present

"I will always be present."

Affirmation: "I will always be present."

Upon completion of Detox 20 - Detox 27, let's gather our thoughts, feelings, and emotions.

My Transitional Thoughts:

1. Reflection

My Detox 20 - Detox 27 summary:

Detox 20 - Detox 27 showed me that I needed to authentically learn about me. This is a stepping stone to accepting me, who I am, what I stand for, and what I am about.

Reflective Prompts:

What did I learn about inner peace?

I am not perfect. Embracing the "NOW" is new to me and will require work. I will need to trust myself that learning a new way of approaching life is okay.

2. Restorative Practices

- Affirmation Meditation:
  - Sit quietly and repeat the affirmation: "I AM PRESENT." Focus on each word and let it sink in.

Your Transitional Thoughts:

1. Reflection

Summarize your thoughts from Detox 20 - Detox 27:

_____

_____

_____

_____

_____

Reflective Prompts:

What did you learn about inner peace?

_____

_____

_____

_____

_____

_____

_____

2. Restorative Practices

- Affirmation Meditation:
    - Sit quietly and repeat the affirmation: "I AM PRESENT."
      Focus on each word and let it sink in.

Preparing for the Next Phase: Self-Discovery

In the next phase, we'll focus on self-discovery. Think about how empowered you will feel with a richer understanding of you.

- Action Step:
  - What does it mean to have a great understanding of yourself?

_____

_____

_____

_____

_____

Scan QR Code for an audio introduction.

Self-Discovery
Detox 29 - Detox 37

DETOX 29

Be Easy

"I am human. It's okay to make mistakes."

Affirmation: Say this out loud, "I forgive myself. I am worth the change."

My Daily Reflection: "I am too hard on myself."

Personal Story:

On this detox day, I woke up feeling calm and relaxed. This journey is definitely showing me that everything I am writing is interconnected. I am proud of myself for being open, honest, and willing to explore my mind and thoughts. I feel strong and secure about the work I have been putting in.

I have made many mistakes in my life and because of them, I feel horrible at times. I have to remind myself that I am not perfect. I told myself, "Be kind to yourself. Embrace your imperfections. Learn from your mistakes. Be easy on yourself!" I think sometimes I forget, I am human and I am allowed to mess up from time to time.

The fear of failure is challenging to me. I am always afraid of what could happen if I am not prepared. Sometimes, I push myself too hard to the point of exhaustion. I keep going until the task is completed or the goal is accomplished. Moving at an aggressive pace would often cause me to neglect my well-being.

No longer will I do this. Moving forward, I will pace myself. I will learn from my mistakes by assessing the situation, exploring all options, and understand that I did my best.

Reflective Prompts:

Close your eyes. Breathe. Relax your mind. Be honest.

Are you hard on yourself? How do you respond to your mistakes? How do you feel when you make a mistake?

Your Daily Reflection:

What came up for you when you read today's reflection and my personal story? Write a sentence about your thoughts and feelings.

_____

_____

_____

_____

_____

Your Personal Story:

Write a short paragraph about your reflection. If you need more space, refer to your Companion Journal.

_____

_____

_____

_____

_____

_____

_____

You Know Yourself:

What prescription would you write for yourself? What do you need to change, add, or remove to help you with negative thoughts, or triggers?

_____

_____

_____

_____

_____

_____

My Action:

My action from today's detox: I took time to explore why I am hard on myself and afraid to make a mistake. I was homeless in my teenage years and that had a profound impact on me. I promised myself that I would never experience that scenario again. Now, what I have to tell myself is that I no longer have to fear that experience because I have a better outlook on life, professional skills, and am now responsible for myself.

Your Action:

1. Are you self-critical? Explore why you are so hard on yourself. Is this something you need to change? What does that look like for you?

2. Find a quote, scripture, or mantra that you like and write it down. Place it where you can see it and when you need it, you will be able to reference it.

DETOX 30

Find your Rhythm

"Move to the beat that makes your heart smile."

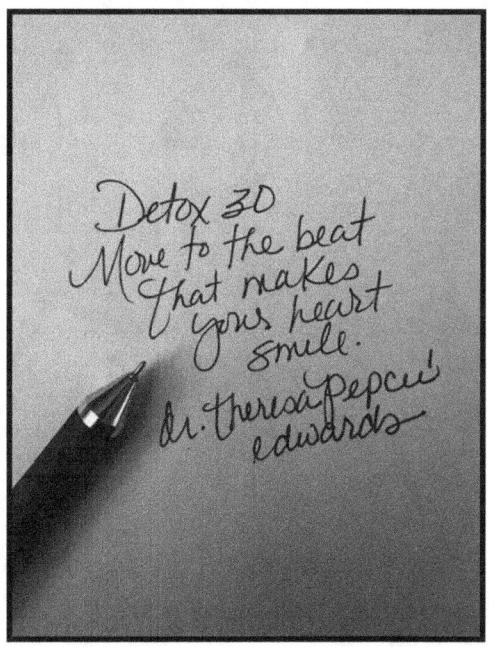

Affirmation: Say this out loud, "I forgive myself. I am worth the change."

My Daily Reflection: "Do what makes me happy."

Personal Story:

Today is different. I woke up without a thought on my mind or a bruised heart. It feels good to confidently tell myself, "I am okay, it's okay, everything will be okay."

I am determined to beat the unexplainable pain that appears unexpectedly. I need to be prepared, have a plan to help me stay emotionally well. What's my prescription? Do things that bring me joy, peace, and happiness... activities that are positive and good for me. I need a *Rhythm Plan*.

Finding my rhythm is putting things in place that work for me. Creating a space that feels safe and soothing. I am extremely careful to not let other people's opinions influence my thinking or decision making.

When I feel good, I do better. I make excellent decisions. It feels good to be in a place to not expect or depend on people to give me what I need.

Dancing to my own beat reminds me that I exist and despite what I have been through, I have purpose.

Reflective Prompts:

Close your eyes. Breathe. Relax your mind. Be honest.

What makes you happy? Are there roadblocks to your happiness? How will you deal with them?

Your Daily Reflection:

What came up for you when you read today's reflection and my personal story? Write a sentence about your thoughts and feelings.

_____

_____

_____

_____

_____

Your Personal Story:

Write a short paragraph about your reflection. If you need more space, refer to your Companion Journal.

_____

_____

_____

_____

_____

_____

_____

You Know Yourself:

What prescription would you write for yourself? What do you need to change, add, or remove to help you with negative thoughts, or triggers?

_____

_____

_____

_____

_____

_____

_____

My Action:

My action from today's detox: I created my own *Rhythm Plan* to help me stay focused, on track and have good mental health. My *Rhythm Plan* includes exercising, listening to music, dancing, and writing once per week about things I am grateful for.

Your Action:

1. Create your *Rhythm Plan*. What are some things that make you happy? Assess your list and ensure that what you listed affects you in a positive manner. List 5 - 10 things you are grateful for, then read the list as often as you like.

2. Find a quote, scripture, or mantra that you like and write it down. Place it where you can see it and when you need it, refer to it.

DETOX 31

All the "SELFS"

"You are one of a kind, a unique
individual; accept who you are."

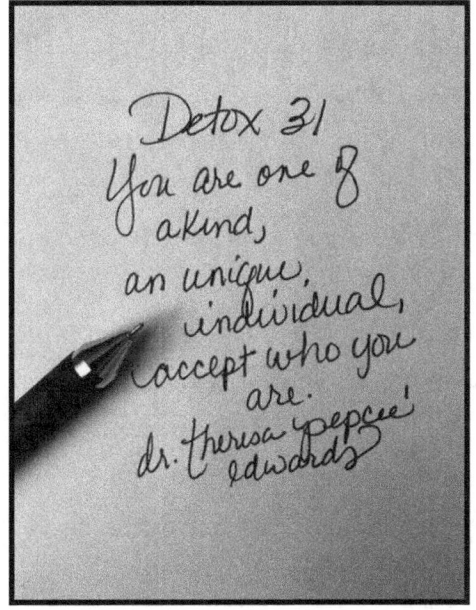

Affirmation: Say this out loud, "I forgive myself. I am worth the change."

My Daily Reflection: "I want to be someone else."

Personal Story:

I remember always wanting to be someone else, anyone other than me. I felt this way for a long time. It started when I was a child experiencing abuse. I would go to school and wish I was another child, especially if they appeared to be happy and had a lot of friends.

Going to school was stressful because I never had decent clothing or shoes. I would see other children who were dressed nicely and talking about things they were doing or what their mom or dad had done for them, etc. These were things I yearned to have in my life. I would spend time daydreaming about being someone else.

As I became older, I yearned for it even more. I did not like myself because of all the things I had experienced, all the pain I carried, the lack of understanding of why life had to be so hard; experiencing break ups did not help. My perception of myself was not the best and my self-esteem was extremely low. I liked some things about me, such as how smart and determined I was, but I did not love me.

For today's detox, I wanted to explore myself, my identity, and gain a deeper sense of who I am. I asked myself, "Do you like who you are?" The answer, "YESSSSS!" This was a much different response from how I felt early on in my life.

But, because I needed to do this detox, it meant I still had some exploring to do. I decided to explore the "SELFS" and the words associated with this and how I felt about them. I choose Self-Esteem, Self-Efficacy, Self-Doubt, Self-Image, and Self-Confidence.

Reflective Prompts:

Close your eyes. Breathe. Relax your mind. Be honest.

How do you really feel about yourself? Do you like who you are? Do you love yourself?

Your Daily Reflection:

What came up for you when you read today's reflection and my personal story? Write a sentence about your thoughts and feelings.

_____

_____

_____

_____

_____

Your Personal Story:

Write a short paragraph about your reflection. If you need more space, refer to your Companion Journal.

_____

_____

_____

_____

_____

_____

_____

_____

You Know Yourself:

What prescription would you write for yourself? What do you need to change, add, or remove to help you with negative thoughts, or triggers?

_____

_____

_____

_____

_____

_____

_____

My Action:

My action from today's detox: As a child I had a poor self-image and did not like myself. I selected "SELFS" that would help me identify what I needed to improve. I am always seeking ways to be a better person. It's about me being the absolute BEST version of myself.

Your Action:

1. Select 5 "SELFS" to explore or you can use the "SELFS" I selected. Think about how you feel about each of them.

2. Find a quote, scripture, or mantra that you like and write it down. Place it where you can see it and when you need it, you will be able to reference it.

DETOX 32

Openly Observing

"I am in competition with myself."

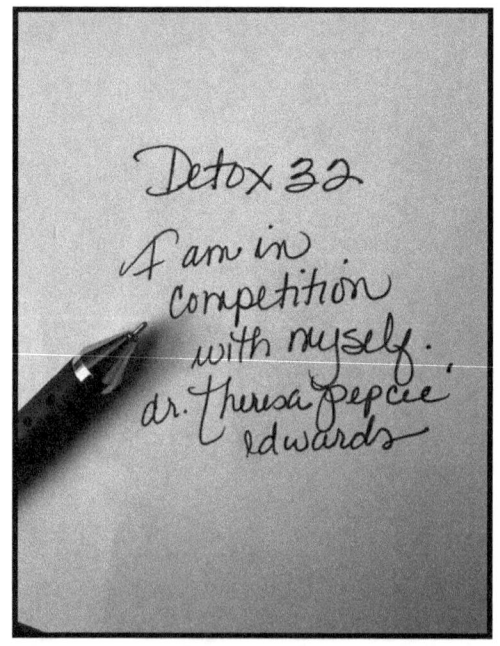

Affirmation: Say this out loud, "I forgive myself. I am worth the change."

My Daily Reflection: "Comparing myself to others is not an option."

Personal Story:

I think I had a false sense of how things should be or go. I also think I brought this pressure to my relationships. I would see how someone else was in their relationship and would compare it to mine or worse, wish I had what they had without recognizing what I was doing.

When I was in my twenties, it was about keeping up—the latest car, clothes, or whatever was trending. I was competing to be dressed the best, drive the best car, and go to the best places. I had an image to uphold and it did not matter what it took.

But through that process, I lost a sense of myself. I needed to be okay with what I had and not concerned with what others had. Even though I was young, some of that carried over into my adulthood. As an adult, I was comparing myself to others. Saying what I should have had caused me anxiety.

Since I was overweight, at least my perception was that I was, I would think a person smaller than me did not have any issues or problems. I think this was my way of escaping how I was really feeling about myself.

As I matured, I learned the value of cherishing what I had and appreciating someone for who they are. I no longer craved having what others had or another person's relationship.

Reflective Prompts:

Close your eyes. Breathe. Relax your mind. Be honest.

Do you compare yourself or your relationships to others? Do you "silently" compete with other people?

Your Daily Reflection:

What came up for you when you read today's reflection and my personal story? Write a sentence about your thoughts and feelings.

_____

_____

_____

_____

_____

Your Personal Story:

Write a short paragraph about your reflection. If you need more space, refer to your Companion Journal.

_____

_____

_____

_____

_____

_____

You Know Yourself:

What prescription would you write for yourself? What do you need to change, add, or remove to help you with negative thoughts, or triggers?

_____

_____

_____

_____

_____

_____

_____

My Action:

My action from today's detox: I wrote down things that I was grateful for and why. I am thankful for everything that I have and am comfortable where I am in my life. I am not hard on myself anymore. I live by my own timeline. I understand when it is time for me to have things, I will.

Your Action:

1. Think about the things you wish you had, why do you want them? Are the reasons because someone else has them? Are you satisfied where you are in your life? Is there anything you can do to change your situation? Create your own elevation plan.

2. Find a quote, scripture, or mantra that you like and write it down. Place it where you can see it and when you need it, you will be able to reference it.

DETOX 33

Who am I? (Personally)

"I am the 'ME' I see."

Affirmation: Say this out loud, "I forgive myself. I am worth the change."

My Daily Reflection: "I love who I have become and am becoming."

Personal Story:

I wrote a quote, "*I am a woman of many dimensions.*" As I grew into womanhood, I was a different woman contingent upon what was happening in my life. When things were not great, I was sad and depressed. When things were going well, I was happy and joyous. But, no matter what my circumstances were, there are traits that remain the same.

I am a person who loves people. I love helping everyone and seeing people win. I want to always make a difference. In 2017, I started a *Warm A Heart* project because I did not want people to feel forgotten during the Thanksgiving holiday. I knew this emotion all too well. I decided to help myself feel good while helping others feel good, too.

I did a video on Facebook, asking for Heart Warmers— people who wanted to help feed a family. To my surprise the Heart Warmers felt like I did and I was told it felt good to help out without the pressure of the donation being expensive. All the families were randomly picked. Each Heart Warmer received a t-shirt and a handwritten card with a special message. The families also received a card with a personalized note written by me.

This is who I am. I love to do kind gestures. I wanted people to know that I did not have to know them, to love them. I know there is someone always thinking about me in this way and I wanted to reciprocate this to others.

I am also a hard worker, go-getter, and determined individual. To help me learn more about myself, I asked people to describe me in one or two words. Here is what I was told: strict, happy, resilient, you persevere, mean, overachiever, beautiful, insightful, introvert, people person, compassionate, funny, action oriented, business minded, no nonsense, empathetic, smart, high achiever, overachiever, caring, anger issues, too sensitive, sweet and shallow.

It was uncomfortable hearing some of the responses. I took this project further by having the conversation of why that person felt that way and was able to bring resolution and better understanding. I found that a person's perception of you could be based on an experience or assumption they had about you.

Reflective Prompts:

Close your eyes. Breathe. Relax your mind. Be honest.

Who are you? What do you think others would say about you? Are you ready to hear the good and bad?

Your Daily Reflection:

What came up for you when you read today's reflection and my personal story? Write a sentence about your thoughts and feelings.

_____

_____

_____

_____

_____

Your Personal Story:

Write a short paragraph about your reflection. If you need more space, refer to your Companion Journal.

_____

_____

_____

_____

_____

_____

_____

You Know Yourself:

What prescription would you write for yourself? What do you need to change, add, or remove to help you with negative thoughts, or triggers?

_____

_____

_____

_____

_____

_____

My Action:

My action from today's detox: I love this part of me, the part that gives and loves without limitations. It is so easy to do this for others, I do it without hesitation. The challenge was learning to give myself what I unconditionally shared with others. Also, it is okay to hear what others say about you, it opens the door to further the conversation to explore clarity and understanding.

Your Action:

1. Think about you; who are you? List your thoughts. Next, ask 10 or more people to describe you in 1 or 2 words. Review the responses. Explore your emotions about the responses. Do you need to make changes? Did you learn something new about you?

2. Find a quote, scripture, or mantra that you like and write it down. Place it where you can see it and when you need it, refer to it.

DETOX 34

Professionally

"I am a professional. I give my all,
at all times. Others depend on it."

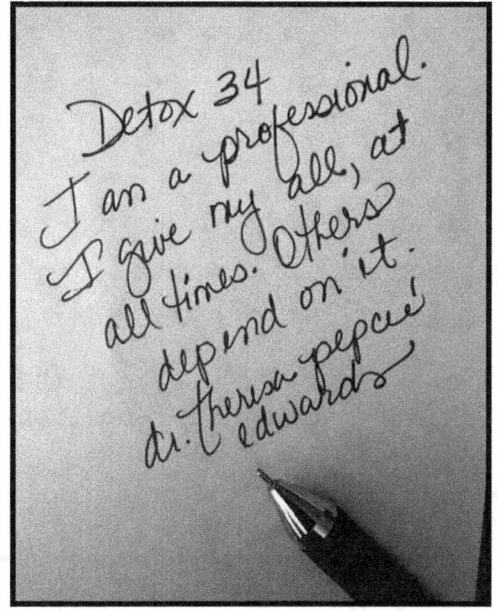

Affirmation: Say this out loud, "I forgive myself. I am worth the change."

My Daily Reflection: "I love who I am at work."

Personal Story:

I absolutely love who I am in a professional environment. Being at work feels like living a different life. It is the one place that I could leave home at home and be who I want to be at work.

My first leadership position took place because of my first supervisor. It was the best decision for my career. Being in leadership allowed me to lead others to achieve the organization's goals. Because I loved people through my leadership, I was able to empower staff, the community, and those seeking the services.

I associate my leadership style with transformational leadership. This leadership style supports what I love doing... motivating, encouraging, and empowering individuals. I try to show up as best as I can because others depend on me. I am really good with separating my personal life or issues from work.

Reflective Prompts:

Close your eyes. Breathe. Relax your mind. Be honest.

Who are you at work? How do you show up? Do you bring your problems to work? If you feel bad, do you take it out on others (co-workers, clients, etc.)?

Your Daily Reflection:

What came up for you when you read today's reflection and my personal story? Write a sentence about your thoughts and feelings.

_____

_____

_____

_____

_____

Your Personal Story:

Write a short paragraph about your reflection. If you need more space, refer to your Companion Journal.

_____

_____

_____

_____

_____

_____

_____

_____

You Know Yourself:

What prescription would you write for yourself? What do you need to change, add, or remove to help you with negative thoughts, or triggers?

_____

_____

_____

_____

_____

_____

_____

My Action:

My action from today's detox: Throughout my life, professionally and personally, I have received so many cards, letters, and messages (written and verbally) expressing my compassion for others. I decided to read each correspondence, and would like to share one with you.

> Dear One,
> I never thought I miss a colleague as much as I'll miss you. You came into our lives and improved the lives of every child you touched. You even improved the lives of those that worked with you. Theresa; you have a gift, a story that you must share with the world.... Make that a part of your mission... and we will be the better because of it;... because of you! Love to you & your family Good fortune forever...

Reading this card reminds me why I love people and being a leader. I consider myself as a change agent that was born to make a difference. In leadership, I am able to ensure that whatever program or business I am overseeing is delivering quality services with dignity and respect.

P.S. I know my ex-coworker would be proud, along with many others, because I am finally telling my story.

Your Action:

1. Conduct an assessment of who you are at work. Do you like who you are? What are things that you can change or enhance that will help you to be a better professional?

2.   Find a quote, scripture, or mantra that you like and write it down. Place it where you can see it and when you need it, you will be able to reference it.

DETOX 35

Family (Your Role)

"Family is your ALL."

Affirmation: Say this out loud, "I forgive myself. I am worth the change."

My Daily Reflection: "I changed my path so that my children could have a better journey."

Personal Story:

When I was pregnant with my eldest child, my life was not great. I had dropped out of high school, was living with my friends, unemployed, and did not have transportation. The father and I had broken up and he did not want anything to do with my child or me. The rejection pushed me into depression. Coupled with this, I had to apply for state assistance and the worker belittled me. She made me feel less than human, and ashamed for being unable to take care of my child. I will always be grateful to my ex-husband for embracing my eldest child. He has never called her his stepdaughter.

My first born is the reason why I started to change my life. I did not want to bring her into a world that did not have hopes and dreams.

My children and grandchildren are what's most important to me. As the matriarch of my family, I have a responsibility to be a role model. Everything I do is for them. I have to demonstrate that they can be anything they want to be, they can achieve all they desire, and they must keep pushing despite what they are going through.

Even as I went through the detox for me, it was also for them. I needed to explore my pain to help me to always be my best self.

Every day, I strive to ensure that my path, whether it is professional or personal, is always headed in an upward direction. I always send them messages of how proud I am of them, I tell them that I love them, and I explain that they could never disappoint me. I encourage them to do what makes them happy. Here is a biblical concept that I teach them: in 2 Thessalonians 3:10, it states, "For even when we were with you, this we commanded you, that if any would not work, neither should he eat." With this understanding they WILL make it.

Reflective Prompts:

Close your eyes. Breathe. Relax your mind. Be honest.

What is your role in your family? Do you feel like you are giving your family the best version of you? Are you a role model?

Your Daily Reflection:

What came up for you when you read today's reflection and my personal story? Write a sentence about your thoughts and feelings.

_____

_____

_____

_____

_____

Your Personal Story:

Write a short paragraph about your reflection. If you need more space, refer to your Companion Journal.

_____

_____

_____

_____

_____

_____

_____

You Know Yourself:

What prescription would you write for yourself? What do you need to change, add, or remove to help you with negative thoughts, or triggers?

_____

_____

_____

_____

_____

_____

My Action:

My action from today's detox: I listed what I appreciated about my family. I listed what I think each of them needed from me. Then, I had a conversation with them to discuss what I had listed.

I wanted to know if what I had listed was in alignment with what they needed.

Your Action:

1. List what you appreciate about your family. What do you think they need from you? Have a conversation with your family members to discuss what you listed and to ask them if that's what they need.

2. Find a quote, scripture, or mantra that you like and write it down. Place it where you can see it and when you need it, you will be able to reference it.

DETOX 36
Relationships (Intentional Connections)
"Life is about stepping outside yourself to SEE yourself."

Affirmation: Say this out loud, "I forgive myself. I am worth the change."

My Daily Reflection: "I am going to explore how I show up in my relationships with men."

Personal Story:

Today's detox is a challenge for me. But it is something that has to be done. They say if you want something different, you have to do something you have never done. I definitely want a different outcome in this area.

I am examining a man's impression of me, or more so things that I have been told. I have been told that I am too emotional. I am not sure what that means. I have noticed that when changes are happening, and I discover that I am not "it" and the relationship is ending, a part of me panics and tries to hold on even tighter. I want to avoid the feeling of rejection and failure.

This is what I wanted to change. When it is ending, I must realize that it is supposed to happen. When I feel the change, I have to understand that I cannot control how the other person feels about me, even if I do not understand why; it's okay to let go. I will live. I had to learn that I was living before they came into my life and I will live after they have exited. Hmmmm… this is easier to write than to do. I can do it though because the feeling from a break up does not last forever.

Fear also holds me back in relationships. I am afraid that if I show all of myself that that's too much. I have been told that I give too much with almost every relationship. In other words, I do too much. My explanation for this was that I have been independently managing a household that includes a child. I have to multi-task, plan ahead, maintain my car and home—not because I want to but because I have to. They say that I am too busy, that I don't need anything, and that I've GOT it! For this reason, over time, I learned to hide parts of myself.

This is what I want to change as well. If I have to hide myself, then HE is not for me.

Reflective Prompts:

Close your eyes. Breathe. Relax your mind. Be honest.

Who are you in relationships? Can you connect your life experiences to who you are in relationships?

Your Daily Reflection:

What came up for you when you read today's reflection and my personal story? Write a sentence about your thoughts and feelings.

_____

_____

_____

_____

_____

Your Personal Story:

Write a short paragraph about your reflection. If you need more space, refer to your Companion Journal.

_____

_____

_____

_____

_____

_____

_____

_____

You Know Yourself:

What prescription would you write for yourself? What do you need to change, add, or remove to help you with negative thoughts, or triggers?

_____

_____

_____

_____

_____

_____

_____

My Action:

My action from today's detox: This detox has helped me explore and understand my emotions. I am more aware of the "why" and now have strategies to help me stay emotionally healthy.

As a single person, I gave myself a few tasks to do: (1) I ended all relationships that were not benefiting me. I wanted a new start. I allowed myself time to explore my emotions. (2) I promised to go on outings or attend 4 events per month. I needed to meet new people. (3) I promised myself that each time I leave the house, I would smell and look my best. This made me feel good and confident.

If I were in a committed relationship, the tasks I would do include: (1) Talking to my partner about our relationship (2) Asking him if there is anything he thinks I should work on (3) Examining if I am providing what he needs (4) Expressing my needs and (5) Showing up as the best version of myself everyday.

Your Action:

1. Think about who you are in your relationships. Think about what you have been told. Do you need to change anything? List a few tasks that will help you to develop or sustain strong positive relationships.

2. Find a quote, scripture, or mantra that you like and write it down. Place it where you can see it and when you need it, you will be able to reference it.

TRANSITIONAL: DETOX 37
Self-Identity

"I must learn to define myself."

Affirmation: "I must learn to define myself."

Upon completion of Detox 29 - Detox 36, let's gather our thoughts, feelings, and emotions.

My Transitional Thoughts:

1. Reflection

My Detox 29 - Detox 36 summary:

I am valuable. Sometimes, I forget that because of what I have gone through.

Reflective Prompts:

What did I learn about self-discovery?

Before I can define myself to others or express my needs to others, I must know who I am.

2. Restorative Practices

- Affirmation Meditation:
  - Sit quietly and repeat the affirmation: "I AM UNIQUE. I AM SPECIAL. I AM WORTHY." Focus on each word and let it sink in.

Your Transitional Thoughts:

1. Reflection

Summarize your thoughts from Detox 29 - Detox 36:

_____

_____

_____

_____

Reflective Prompts:

What did you learn about self-discovery?

_____

_____

_____

_____

2. Restorative Practices

- Affirmation Meditation:
  - Sit quietly and repeat the affirmation: "I AM UNIQUE. I AM SPECIAL. I AM WORTHY." Focus on each word and let it sink in.

Preparing for the Next Phase: Financial Empowerment

In the next phase, we'll focus on financial empowerment. Think about how you are financially responsible.

- Action Step:
  - Write down your financial goals. Next to each one, describe why the goal is important.

Scan QR Code for an audio introduction.

Financial Empowerment
Balancing Benjamin
Detox 38 - Detox 39

DETOX 38

Feelings and Finances

"Feelings fuel my funds."

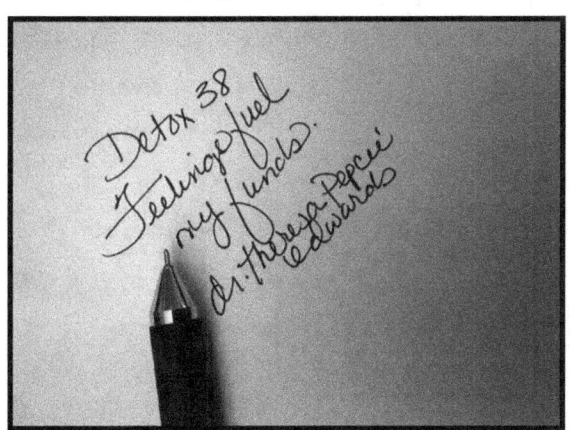

Affirmation: Say this out loud, "I forgive myself. I am worth the change."

My Daily Reflection: "I hate feeling financially uncomfortable."

Personal Story:

My mother did the best with what she had. When you hear that statement, you already know there were financial challenges. I remember feeling uncomfortable all the time because I did not have school clothes. I only had 5 pairs of pants for the entire school year. I would alternate with different tops.

Over time, the inside of my jeans would become worn out, creating holes. I would sew the hole only to have it burst during the school day. I would then tie my jacket around my waist to try and hide the hole. I felt uncomfortable, embarrassed, and self-conscious.

Because of those emotions, as I became an adult, I feel like my focus was always on "chasing" money. I never wanted to be without it I had not figured out how to get an abundance of it. I always felt like I was struggling and did not have adequate income to create a good quality of life.

Even though I had graduated with my Master's degree, I made $29,000 a year. This was not enough to take care of two children and myself. Once again, I was feeling uncomfortable, not embarrassed but distressed. This was affecting my mental health. I was upset and sad about my situation.

To avoid feeling financially stressed, I reviewed my finances monthly. If everything had been taken care of and I had $20.00

left over, I would be happy. However, I am not going to stop there, I am actually now able to have a savings plan. I told myself, "Girl, no amount is too large or too small, JUST start!"

Another aspect that I reviewed on today's detox was my credit report. I remember when I felt disgusted about my credit score. I learned that your credit score will fluctuate depending on what's going on in your life. Every year, I would order my free credit report and dispute accounts as applicable.

Part of taking care of myself included having good financial health. It also included being conscious of my mood and how it can determine my financial decisions.

Reflective Prompts:

Close your eyes. Breathe. Relax your mind. Be honest.

How is your financial health? Are you a person that shops based on your mood? Is shopping a coping mechanism for you?

Your Daily Reflection:

What came up for you when you read today's reflection and my personal story? Write a sentence about your thoughts and feelings.

_____

_____

_____

_____

_____

Your Personal Story:

Write a short paragraph about your reflection. If you need more space, refer to your Companion Journal.

_____

_____

_____

_____

_____

_____

_____

You Know Yourself:

What prescription would you write for yourself? What do you need to change, add, or remove to help you with negative thoughts, or triggers?

_____

_____

_____

_____

_____

_____

My Action:

My action from today's detox: I went on a financial diet. I discontinued things that I did not need or was not utilizing, such as subscriptions and memberships. Next, I ordered my credit report, reviewed, and disputed accounts.

Your Action:

1. Examine your relationship with your finances. Examine how your mood impacts your spending. Start a financial diet. Review your bills and debts; cut where you can. Order your credit report. Review and dispute where applicable.

2. Find a quote, scripture, or mantra that you like and write it down. Place it where you can see it and when you need it, you will be able to reference it.

DETOX 39

Finances + Goals = YOU

"Financial stability can happen, if you do the work."

Affirmation: Say this out loud, "I forgive myself. I am worth the change."

My Daily Reflection: "I deserve financial freedom."

Personal Story:

Financial goals are critical to having stable finances. This includes knowing where every dollar I earn goes and what my credit report shows. Setting goals to improve my financial health required me setting achievable milestones. I decided to set small goals to reach it.

When I began my financial diet, I took away spending and added it to my savings plan. For example, I had at least 6 streaming apps. I discontinued 4, which will save me $45 per month. I put that money in my savings. I also canceled monthly and annual memberships. I think I had a tendency of keeping things active with the "just in case" mentality.

Being stress free from financial turmoil may mean something different to you. Setting financial goals may also have a different meaning. Nonetheless, do not be afraid to face your finances and challenge yourself to do better. For me, it's not about being rich. It's about having peace, enjoying life, savoring the small things, and being happy.

Reflective Prompts:

Close your eyes. Breathe. Relax your mind. Be honest.

Are you happy with your finances? Do you have financial goals?

Your Daily Reflection:

What came up for you when you read today's reflection and my personal story? Write a sentence about your thoughts and feelings.

_____

_____

_____

_____

_____

Your Personal Story:

Write a short paragraph about your reflection. If you need more space, refer to your Companion Journal.

_____

_____

_____

_____

_____

_____

_____

_____

You Know Yourself:

What prescription would you write for yourself? What do you need to change, add, or remove to help you with negative thoughts, or triggers?

_____

_____

_____

_____

_____

_____

_____

My Action:

My action from today's detox: I purchased a notebook for tracking my financial goals. I set goals in the following areas: Savings, Checking, and Activities. I also set goals for my credit score and outstanding debt.

Your Action:

1. Define what financial stability means to you and your finances. Create a financial diet. Reallocate funds to your saving plan, if applicable. Write 3 financial goals with a timeline and review schedule.

2. Find a quote, scripture, or mantra that you like and write it down. Place it where you can see it and when you need it, you will be able to reference it.

Scan QR Code for an audio introduction.

DETOX 40

Think, Believe, Achieve

I AM

DETOX 40

Tomorrow

"Always believe that your tomorrow
will be greater than your today."

Affirmation: "Always believe that your tomorrow will be greater than your today."

Upon completion of Detox 1 - Detox 39, let's reflect on each day. Think about the affirmations, personal stories, the prescriptions, and Action! Think about your growth, the changes, and motivation needed to work daily on yourself.

My Transitional Thoughts:

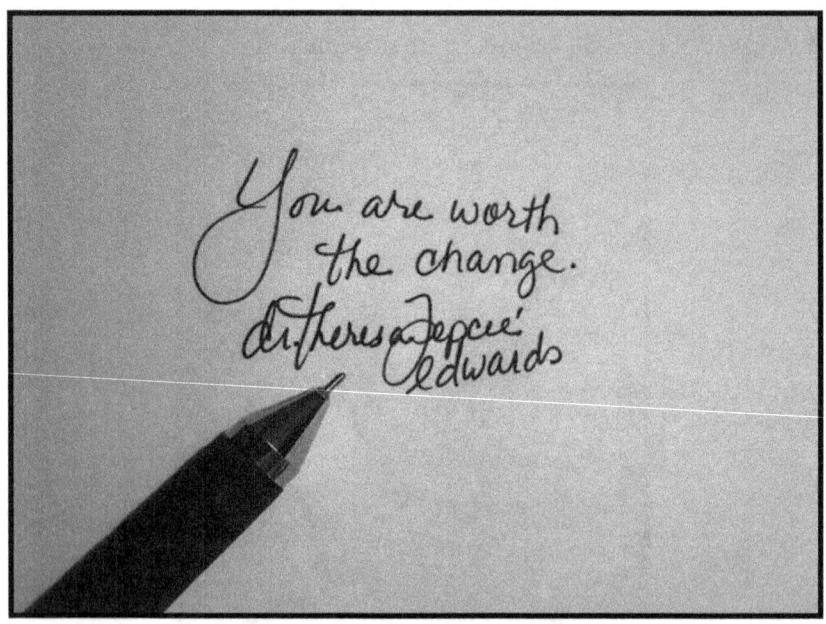

1. Reflection

My Detox 1- Detox 39 summary:

This was an emotional journey that forced me to be honest, authentic, and brave. I faced my innermost thoughts and feelings. I feel more focused, determined, and have a better understanding of me. I pushed through my own fears and anxiety. I also feel more at peace, especially since I am more organized and in control of all areas of my life.

I am grateful for the following:

- My heart belongs 100% to me.

- I unconditionally love myself.

- I am not **inappropriately** attached to anyone mentally, physically, or emotionally.

- My mind is decluttered.

- I have a financial plan.

- The unexplainable pain is gone!

- I am at peace.

Reflective Prompts:

What did I learn about my 40-day human detox journey?

"I am in competition with myself." Loving myself authentically is the greatest gift I can give myself. Being held captive to the past, holding on to harmful memories, or spending time trying to figure out the why is catastrophic to my emotional well-being. "My mind is not a space for hurtful storage."

"Dry tears are just as painful as wet ones." Healing occurs when you face your trauma, forgive, and let go. I also learned that I still need work dealing with my sexual assault because I have not forgiven him. I am at peace but that is not enough to be 100% healed.

I also learned that if I wanted to change how I felt about my past, I needed to do the work in the future such as I have done with completing my 40-day human detox. Now, when I think about my past, I am happy because I am living the results of my work. I am no longer a supporting character in my own life—I am the star, the main character, the director, and author. I am worthy!

I am a FIGHTER. I AM WORTH THE CHANGE!

2. Restorative Practices

- Affirmation Meditation:
    - Sit quietly and repeat the affirmation: "I AM WORTH THE CHANGE." Focus on each word and let it sink in.

Your Transitional Thoughts:

1. Reflection

Summarize your thoughts from Detox 1 - Detox 39:

_____

_____

_____

_____

_____

_____

_____

_____

Reflective Prompts:

What did you learn about your 40-day detox journey?

_____

_____

_____

_____

_____

_____

_____

2. Restorative Practices

- Affirmation Meditation:
    - Sit quietly and repeat the affirmation: "I AM WORTH THE CHANGE." Focus on each word and let it sink in.

In the next phase, we'll focus on sustaining and maintaining. Think about how you will sustain the work you have done and maintain who you have become.

- Action Steps:
    - List 3 things that you are proud of that you accomplished while on your path to healing, inner peace and self-discovery.
    - Write a letter to yourself acknowledging how far you have come, things you will implement to sustain and maintain the work you have done, how you will encourage yourself to be the best version of yourself, and how you will celebrate the new you.

Congratulations on completing your 40-Day Human Detox! Your journey of reflection and growth deserves to be celebrated.

Keep the inspiration going—treat yourself to a special t-shirt and mug as a reminder that:

YOU ARE WORTH THE CHANGE!

Place your order today and be part of our community! Visit the link or scan the QR Code to shop now: www.40dayhumandetox.com Send in your picture rocking your t-shirt or sipping from your mug to be featured on our website! **Email: admin@40dayhumandetox.com**

Bonus: Pepcee's Powerful Weapon List (2011, Revised 2025)
This is a list that I live by. I read it almost every day, when I feel overwhelmed, or just need to be encouraged.

1. Options

    One of the most powerful weapons you can have in your life is to know that you have the POWER to have OPTIONS!

2. Authority

    The second most powerful weapon you have is AUTHORITY! You have the AUTHORITY to be the leader in your life. Stop letting the wrong people dictate your destiny.

3. Strength

    The third most powerful weapon you have is STRENGTH! You have the STRENGTH to cast out negativity, drama, and MESS.

4. Conquer

    The fourth most powerful weapon you have is the ability to CONQUER! Pounce on, stamp down, and take possession of what you want! Command, dominate and CONQUER your desires. Delete, erase, and minus those that stand in your way!

5. Stand

    The fifth most powerful weapon you have is the ability to STAND! You can STAND as tall as you want because YOU are a child of God! Walk by FAITH not by SIGHT! Hint: You cannot do it sitting down! STAND, STAND TALL, STEP, and WALK. Walk into your destiny.

6. Appreciate

    The sixth most powerful weapon you have is the ability to APPRECIATE! You cannot reach back into yesterday or reach forward into tomorrow. But you can APPRECIATE today!

7. Love

    The seventh most powerful weapon you have is the ability to LOVE! Loving yourself is the greatest gift and loving others is unconditional.

8. Delete

    The eighth most powerful weapon you have is the ability to DELETE! Delete all negativity, people who are draining, situations that are hurtful, environments that are not thriving and negative self-talk. You are what you keep!

9. Forgiveness

    The ninth most powerful weapon you have is the ability to FORGIVE! Forgive those who betrayed, hurt, or harmed you. Let it go and lose the weight!

10. Apologize

    The tenth most powerful weapon you have is the ability to say I AM SORRY! We have all SAID and DONE wrong things to people. Set people free. Apologize and mean it!

ABOUT THE AUTHOR

Dr. Theresa Pepcee' Edwards

Beacon of Hope, Advocate, Speaker, and Leader

Dr. Theresa Pepcee' Edwards is a powerhouse of resilience, leadership, and inspiration. With over 25 years of experience in both the nonprofit and for-profit sectors, she is deeply committed to empowering others to rise above adversity and reach their full potential. Her

life's mission is rooted in the unwavering belief that no matter where you come from or what you've been through, IT IS POSSIBLE to create the life you desire.

Her journey is one of incredible transformation. After enduring sexual, physical, and verbal abuse, experiencing homelessness at 14, losing both parents within weeks of each other, and dropping out of high school, Dr. Edwards refused to let her circumstances define her. She rebuilt her life through perseverance, faith, and education—proving that obstacles are merely stepping stones to greatness.

A dynamic transformational speaker, educator, and author, Dr. Edwards has been sharing her story and inspiring audiences since 1999. She has spoken at countless workshops and conferences, including her keynote address at the 2018 Wayne State African American Graduation Celebration, one of the proudest moments of her career. Whether speaking to an intimate group or a packed auditorium, she brings authenticity, encouragement, and a presence that ignites hope.

Dr. Edwards holds a doctorate of Business Administration (2017), a Master's in Social Work (1999), a Bachelor's in Social Work (1998), an Associate of Arts (1996), and a GED (1992). As an advocate for personal growth, healing, and transformation, she has spent decades helping individuals break through barriers and take control of their futures.

Now, as the author of *The 40-Day Human Detox*, Dr. Edwards shares her powerful story and life lessons to inspire others to embrace their struggles, discover their strength, and walk boldly into their purpose.

Through her voice, her work, and her unwavering faith, Dr. Theresa Pepcee' Edwards continues to be a beacon of light, reminding the world that no matter what challenges life brings, IT IS POSSIBLE and YOU ARE WORTH THE CHANGE.

If you'd like to book Dr. Theresa Pepcee' Edwards for speaking engagements, seminars, interviews or for any other press-related inquiries: Email: admin@40dayhumandetox.com or Visit: www.40dayhumandetox.com

www.ingramcontent.com/pod-product-compliance
Lightning Source LLC
Chambersburg PA
CBHW060141130626
46556CB00006B/2435